P·O·E·M·S
FOR PLEASURE

P·O·E·M·S
FOR PLEASURE

Introduced by
PHILLIP SCHOFIELD

Introductory Poems specially written by
JOHN HEGLEY

HAMLYN

Illustrations by:
Victor Ambrus, Rowan Barnes-Murphy,
Robin Lawrie, Keith Rawling, Amelia Rosato,
Meg Rutherford, Gill Tomblin.

Additional black and white illustrations
courtesy of *Handbook of Early Advertising Art* by Clarence P. Hornung
published by Dover Publications, Inc. New York.

Designed by Kit Johnson
Editor Gillian Denton

Photograph Phillip Schofield by Simon Fowler
Photograph John Hegley by Alison Ruddock

This edition 1989 published by The Hamlyn Publishing Group,
Michelin House, 81 Fulham Road, London SW3 6RB.

© Copyright this edition 1989 The Hamlyn Publishing Group,
a division of The Octopus Publishing Group Limited.

ISBN 0 600 56686 2
Printed in Spain

CONTENTS

INTRODUCTION

I've just been re-introduced to an old friend I haven't seen for years – 17 to be precise. The last time we met was in Cornwall, at school. It was raining outside and the lesson inside was getting almost as dull as the day. Suddenly, the teacher, Mr Hayes, had a spark of educational genius and decided to lighten the atmosphere, which had been made heavy and humid by wet anoraks drying steamily on the radiator. And that is how I was first introduced to my friend. It was only a brief acquaintance, in fact only a couple of hours' discussion in the classroom, forgotten in the frenzied dash to the canteen, through the slivers of icy rain that came at me sideways and undid all the radiator's hard work.

Later, I remembered, perhaps not everything, but certainly enough for me to know that if by chance we ever came across one another again, I'd positively wallow in the knowledge that I could fill in the gaps that had long since been forgotten. And here we are, years down the road, or more correctly, track, re-acquainted, all the shady areas filled and the memory sharp again. I'd love you to meet this friend of mine called ... *From A Railway Carriage* (You'll find him on page 19).

So many times I've sat on a train, my breath steaming up the window as I watched the world flying by and wished I could remember all sixteen lines of that wonderful poem but never being able to get past the fourth. I was so pleased when I found it in this book.

Why is it that when we are young we can soak up poetry and rhymes? 'Sing a Song of Sixpence' and 'Ring a Ring of Roses' delighted me when I was younger although I did not have a clue what they were all about. For me, like so many other kids, the magic of poetry was lost the moment I started to study it, to dissect and analyse it. What I forgot to do was enjoy it. Everything got so complicated. Poetry was too difficult to inter- pret and had nothing to do with everyday life, so I moved on and left it with a big sticker marked 'BORING'. What a mistake. It was only years later that I realised how much I had missed out on. 'Read to enjoy' – that's my motto now.

Poetry purists will probably sniff if I compare this book with pop music, but I am not a purist (and remember the motto). In pop there are always 'Greatest Hits' albums consisting of the best songs, and what we have here, is a poetry 'Greatest Hits'.

Some of the poems surprised me – one of the nice things about poetry. Byron's *Italy versus England* could have been written yesterday, and I had not realised that Wordsworth's *Daffodils* with the first line that everyone knows, 'I wandered lonely as a cloud', was such a beautiful poem.

We all understand what Adrian Mitchell was talking about in *Back in the Playground Blues*, and I think that *School Dinners* was probably written by a child, it's so true. Brian Patten's *The Trouble with My Sister* will definitely ring a few bells with boys whose sisters borrow their skateboards and puncture their footballs. Other great well-known poems include Rudyard Kipling's *If* and William Blake's instantly recognisable *The Tyger*. There are childhood favourites like *The Owl and the Pussy-Cat*, the epic *The Pied Piper of Hamelin*, and *A Red Red Rose* which you can send to someone you fancy! I am going to send this book to a mate of mine who only knows the first few lines of *Kubla Khan*; now maybe he will save us all the torture of his edited version and learn the whole thing.

It is impossible for me to pick favourites, but Roger McGough's *The Leader* is me, I am sure. Spike Milligan's *The Terns* is . . . short!

Poems for Pleasure is meant for just that. Tap into the magic and you will experience a whole new world, and find yourself as instantly and miraculously transported as I was. Enjoy, and remember when your anorak is drying:

> The cow is of the bovine ilk;
> One end is moo, the other, milk.

OGDEN NASH

WHEN WE WERE YOUNG

when we weren't women and men
when we were fourteen five and ten
when we spent our lives in a den
when we were children
that's when

maggie and milly and molly and may

maggie and milly and molly and may
went down to the beach (to play one day)

and maggie discovered a shell that sang
so sweetly she couldn't remember her troubles, and

milly befriended a stranded star
whose rays five languid fingers were;

and molly was chased by a horrible thing
which raced sideways while blowing bubbles: and

may came home with a smooth round stone
as small as a world and as large as alone.

For whatever we lost (like a you or a me)
it's always ourselves we find in the sea

e e cummings

At the Seaside

When I was down beside the sea
A wooden spade they gave to me
To dig the sandy shore.
My holes were empty like a cup,
In every hole the sea came up
Till it could come no more.

ROBERT LOUIS STEVENSON

A Boy's Song

Where the pools are bright and deep,
Where the grey trout lies asleep,
Up the river and o'er the lea –
That's the way for Billy and me.

Where the blackbird sings the latest,
Where the hawthorn blooms the sweetest,
Where the nestlings chirp and flee –
That's the way for Billy and me.

Where the mowers mow the cleanest,
Where the hay lies thick and greenest,
There to trace the homeward bee –
That's the way for Billy and me.

Where the hazel bank is steepest,
Where the shadow falls the deepest,
Where the clustering nuts fall free –
That's the way for Billy and me.

There let us walk, there let us play,
Through the meadows, among the hay.
Up the water, and o'er the lea –
That's the way for Billy and me.

JAMES HOGG

17

The Railway Children

When we climbed the slopes of the cutting
We were eye-level with the white cups
Of the telegraph poles and the sizzling wires.

Like lovely freehand they curved for miles
East and miles west beyond us, sagging
Under their burden of swallows.

We were small and thought we knew nothing
Worth knowing. We thought words travelled the wires
In the shiny pouches of raindrops,

Each one seeded full with the light
Of the sky, the gleam of the lines, and ourselves
So infinitesimally scaled

We could stream through the eye of a needle.

SEAMUS HEANEY

From a Railway Carriage

Faster than fairies, faster than witches,
Bridges and houses, hedges and ditches;
And charging along like troops in a battle,
All through the meadows the horses and cattle:
All of the sights of the hill and the plain
Fly as thick as driving rain;
And ever again, in the wink of an eye,
Painted stations whistle by.

Here is a child who clambers and scrambles,
All by himself and gathering brambles;
Here is a tramp who stands and gazes;
And there is the green for stringing the daisies!
Here is a cart run away in the road
Lumping along with man and load;
And here is a mill, and there is a river:
Each a glimpse and gone for ever!

ROBERT LOUIS STEVENSON

Back in the Playground Blues

Dreamed I was in a school playground, I was about four feet high
Yes dreamed I was back in the playground, and standing about four feet high
The playground was three miles long and the playground was five miles wide

It was broken black tarmac with a high fence all around
Broken black dusty tarmac with a high fence running all around
And it had a special name to it, they called it The Killing Ground.

Got a mother and a father, they're a thousand miles away
The Rulers of the Killing Ground are coming out to play
Everyone thinking: who they going to play with today?

  You get it for being Jewish
  Get it for being black
  Get it for being chicken
  Get it for fighting back
  You get it for being big and fat
  Get it for being small
  O those who get it get it and get it
  For any damn thing at all

Sometimes they take a beetle, tear off its six legs one by one
Beetle on its black back rocking in the lunchtime sun
But a beetle can't beg for mercy, a beetle's not half the fun

Heard a deep voice talking, it had that iceberg sound;
"It prepares them for Life" – but I have never found
Any place in my life that's worse than The Killing Ground.

ADRIAN MITCHELL

The Hero

Slowly with bleeding nose and aching wrists
After tremendous use of feet and fists
He rises from the dusty schoolroom floor
And limps for solace to the girl next door
Boasting of kicks and punches, cheers and noise,
And far worse damage done to bigger boys.

ROBERT GRAVES

The Leader

I wanna be the leader
I wanna be the leader
Can I be the leader?
Can I? I can?
Promise? Promise?
Yippee, I'm the leader
I'm the leader

OK what shall we do?

ROGER MCGOUGH

School Dinners

If you stay to school dinners
Better throw them aside;
A lot of kids didn't,
A lot of kids died.

The meat is made of iron,
The spuds are made of steel;
And if that don't get you
The afters will!

UNKNOWN

A Lullaby

Speak roughly to your little boy,
    And beat him when he sneezes.
He only does it to annoy,
    Because he knows it teases.

      Wow! wow! wow!

I speak severely to my boy,
    I beat him when he sneezes;
For he can thoroughly enjoy
    The pepper when he pleases!

      Wow! wow! wow!

LEWIS CARROLL

22

Believing

I don't believe in vampires,
I'll say it loud and clear,
I don't believe in werewolves,
When other folk are near.

I certainly don't believe in ghosts,
All those that do are fools,
And I know for an absolute positive fact,
There are no such things as ghouls.

So why, when it is late at night,
After all that I've just said,
Do vampires, werewolves, ghosts and ghouls
All gather underneath my bed?

The truth, of course, is obvious,
And plain for all to see,
For though I don't believe in *them*,
They all believe in *me!*

WILLIS HALL

When All the World is Young

When all the world is young, lad,
    And all the trees are green;
And every goose a swan, lad,
    And every lass a queen;
Then hey for boot and horse, lad,
    And round the world away;
Young blood must have its course, lad,
    And every dog his day.

When all the world is old, lad,
    And all the trees are brown;
And all the sport is stale, lad,
    And all the wheels run down:
Creep home, and take your place there,
    The spent and maimed among:
God grant you find one face there
    You loved when all was young.

CHARLES KINGSLEY

If –

If you can keep your head when all about you
    Are losing theirs and blaming it on you,
If you can trust yourself when all men doubt you,
    But make allowance for their doubting too;
If you can wait and not be tired by waiting,
    Or being lied about, don't deal in lies,
Or being hated don't give way to hating,
    And yet don't look too good, nor talk too wise:

If you can dream – and not make dreams your master;
    If you can think – and not make thoughts your aim:
If you can meet with Triumph and Disaster
    And treat those two impostors just the same;
If you can bear to hear the truth you've spoken
    Twisted by knaves to make a trap for fools,
Or watch the things you gave your life to, broken,
    And stoop and build 'em up with worn-out tools:

If you can make one heap of all your winnings
    And risk it on one turn of pitch-and-toss,
And lose, and start again at your beginnings
    And never breathe a word about your loss;
If you can force your heart and nerve and sinew
    To serve your turn long after they are gone,
And so hold on when there is nothing in you
    Except the Will which says to them: "Hold on!"

If you can talk with crowds and keep your virtue,
    Or walk with Kings – nor lose the common touch,
If neither foes nor loving friends can hurt you,
    If all men count with you, but none too much;
If you can fill the unforgiving minute
    With sixty seconds' worth of distance run,
Yours is the Earth and everything that's in it,
    And – which is more – you'll be a Man, my son!

RUDYARD KIPLING

ME, MY FAMILY AND OTHER PEOPLE

it's a fair old family gathering
and the guest list isn't small
but even though we've crammed 'em in
there's room for you 'n' all

My Nose

It doesn't breathe;
It doesn't smell;
It doesn't feel
So very well.

I am discouraged
With my nose:
The only thing it
Does is blows.

DOROTHY ALDIS

My Brother Bert

Pets are the hobby of my brother Bert.
He used to go to school with a mouse in his shirt.

His hobby it grew, as some hobbies will,
And grew and GREW and GREW until–

Oh don't breathe a word, pretend you haven't heard.
A simply appalling thing has occurred–

The very thought makes me iller and iller:
Bert's brought home a gigantic gorilla!

If you think that's really not such a scare,
What if it quarrels with his grizzly bear?

You still think you could keep your head?
What if the lion from under the bed

And the four ostriches that deposit
Their football eggs in his bedroom closet

And the aardvark out of his bottom drawer
All danced out and joined in the roar?

What if the pangolins were to caper
Out of their nests behind the wallpaper?

With the fifty sorts of bats
That hang on his hatstand like old hats,

And out of a shoebox the excitable platypus
Along with the ocelot or jungle-cattypus?

The wombat, the dingo, the gecko, the grampus–
How they would shake the house with their rumpus!

Not to forget the bandicoot
Who would certainly peer from his battered old boot.

Why it could be a dreadful day,
And what, oh what, would the neighbours say!

TED HUGHES

The Trouble with My Sister

My little sister was truly awful,
She was really shocking,
She put the budgie in the fridge
And slugs in Mummy's stocking.

She was really awful,
But it was a load of fun
When she stole old Uncle Wilbur's
Double-barrelled gun.

She aimed it at a pork pie
And blew it into bits,
She aimed it at a hamster
That was having fits.

She leapt up on the telly,
She pirouetted on the cat,
She gargled with some jelly
And spat in Grandad's hat.

She ran down the hallway,
She ran across the road,
She dug up lots of little worms
And caught a squirming toad.

She put them in a large pot
And she began to stir,
She added a pint of bat's blood
And some rabbit fur.

She leapt upon the Hoover,
Around the room she went,
Once she had a turned-up nose
But now her nose is bent.

I like my little sister,
There is really just one hitch,
I think my little sister
Has become a little witch.

BRIAN PATTEN

There Was a Little Girl

There was a little girl, who had a little curl
    Right in the middle of her forehead,
And when she was good, she was very, very good,
    But when she was bad she was horrid.

HENRY LONGFELLOW

Aunt Sponge and Aunt Spiker

"I look and smell," Aunt Sponge declared, "as
    lovely as a rose!
Just feast your eyes upon my face, observe my
    shapely nose!
Behold my heavenly silky locks!
And if I take off both my socks
You'll see my dainty toes."
"But don't forget," Aunt Spiker cried, "how much
    your tummy shows!"

Aunt Sponge went red. Aunt Spiker said, "My
    sweet, you cannot win,
Behold MY gorgeous curvy shape, my teeth, my
    charming grin!
Oh, beauteous me! How I adore
My radiant looks! And please ignore
The pimple on my chin."
"My dear old trout!" Aunt Sponge cried out. "You're
    only bones and skin!

"Such loveliness as I possess can only truly shine
In Hollywood!" Aunt Sponge declared. "Oh,
    wouldn't that be fine!
I'd capture all the nations' hearts!
They'd give me all the leading parts!
The stars would all resign!"
"I think you'd make," Aunt Spiker said, "a lovely
    Frankenstein."

ROALD DAHL

Grandad's Glasses

We never used to ask questions
about his glasses.
He needed them to see the telly
and that was that
but then one day
he couldn't see the telly anymore
so he didn't need his glasses.
What were we to do?
It seemed wrong to throw away the glasses
and there was no point in burying them with him
because
a. his eyes were shut
and b. none of us believed in telly after death.
We had a family get together about it
and after the big argument
we came up with two possibilities
a. find someone with glasses like grandad's
and give them the glasses
and b. find someone with glasses like grandad's
and sell them the glasses.

JOHN HEGLEY

Colonel Fazackerley

Colonel Fazackerley Butterworth-Toast
Bought an old castle complete with a ghost,
But someone or other forgot to declare
To Colonel Fazack that the spectre was there.

On the very first evening, while waiting to dine,
The Colonel was taking a fine sherry wine,
When the ghost, with a furious flash and a flare,
Shot out of the chimney and shivered, "Beware!"

Colonel Fazackerley put down his glass
And said, "My dear fellow, that's really first class!
I just can't conceive how you do it at all.
I imagine you're going to a Fancy Dress Ball?"

At this, the dread ghost gave a withering cry.
Said the Colonel (his monocle firm in his eye),
"Now just how you do it I wish I could think.
Do sit down and tell me, and please have a drink."

The ghost in his phosphorous cloak gave a roar
And floated about between ceiling and floor.
He walked through a wall and returned through a pane
And backed up the chimney and came down again. Said the
Colonel, "With laughter I'm feeling quite weak!"
(As trickles of merriment ran down his cheek).
"My house-warming party I hope you won't spurn.
You *must* say you'll come and you'll give us a turn!"

At this, the poor spectre – quite out of his wits –
Proceeded to shake himself almost to bits.
He rattled his chains and he clattered his bones
And he filled the whole castle with mumbles and moans.

But Colonel Fazackerley, just as before,
Was simply delighted and called out, "Encore!"
At which the ghost vanished, his efforts in vain,
And never was seen at the castle again. "Oh dear, what a pity!"
said Colonel Fazack.
"I don't know his name, so I can't call him back."
And then with a smile that was hard to define,
Colonel Fazackerley went in to dine.

CHARLES CAUSLEY

The Pied Piper of Hamelin

Hamelin Town's in Brunswick,
  By famous Hanover city;
The river Weser, deep and wide,
Washes its wall on the southern side;
A pleasanter spot you never spied;
  But, when begins my ditty,
Almost five hundred years ago,
To see the townsfolk suffer so
  From vermin, was a pity.

  Rats!
They fought the dogs and killed the cats,
  And bit the babies in the cradles,
And ate the cheeses out of the vats,
  And licked the soup from the cooks' own ladles,
Split open the kegs of salted sprats,
Made nests inside men's Sunday hats,
And even spoiled the women's chats
      By drowning their speaking
      With shrieking and squeaking
In fifty different sharps and flats.

At last the people in a body
      To the Town Hall came flocking:
"'Tis clear," cried they, "our Mayor's a noddy;
      And as for our Corporation – shocking
To think we buy gowns lined with ermine
For dolts that can't or won't determine
What's best to rid us of our vermin!
You hope, because you're old and obese,
To find in the furry civic robe ease?
Rouse up, sirs! Give your brains a racking
To find the remedy we're lacking,
Or, sure as fate, we'll send you packing!"
At this the Mayor and Corporation
Quaked with a mighty consternation.

An hour they sat in council,
  At length the Mayor broke silence:
"For a guilder I'd my ermine gown sell,
  I wish I were a mile hence!

It's easy to bid one rack one's brain—
I'm sure my poor head aches again,
I've scratched it so, and all in vain.
Oh for a trap, a trap, a trap!"
Just as he said this, what should hap
At the chamber door but a gentle tap?
"Bless us," cried the Mayor, "what's that?"
(With the Corporation as he sat,
Looking little though wondrous fat;
Nor brighter was his eye, nor moister
Than a too-long-opened oyster,
Save when at noon his paunch grew mutinous
For a plate of turtle, green and glutinous)
"Only a scraping of shoes on the mat?
Anything like the sound of a rat
Makes my heart go pit-a-pat!"

"Come in!" the Mayor cried, looking bigger:
And in did come the strangest figure!
His queer long coat from heel to head
Was half of yellow and half of red,
And he himself was tall and thin,
With sharp blue eyes, each like a pin,
And light loose hair, yet swarthy skin,
No tuft on cheek nor beard on chin,
But lips where smiles went out and in;
There was no guessing his kith and kin:
And nobody could enough admire
The tall man and his quaint attire.
Quoth one: "It's as my great-grandsire,
Starting up at the Trump of Doom's tone,
Had walked this way from his painted tombstone!"

He advanced to the council-table:
And, "Please your honours," said he, "I'm able,
By means of a secret charm, to draw
    All creatures living beneath the sun,
    That creep or swim or fly or run,
After me so as you never saw!
And I chiefly use my charm
On creatures that do people harm,
The mole and toad and newt and viper;
And people call me the Pied Piper."

(And here they noticed round his neck
    A scarf of red and yellow stripe,
To match with his coat of the self-same check;
    And at the scarf's end hung a pipe;
And his fingers, they noticed, were ever straying
As if impatient to be playing
Upon this pipe, as low it dangled
Over his vesture so old-fangled.)
"Yet," said he, "poor piper as I am,
In Tartary I freed the Cham,
    Last June, from his huge swarms of gnats;
I eased in Asia the Nizam
    Of a monstrous brood of vampire-bats:
And as for what your brain bewilders,
    If I can rid your town of rats
Will you give me a thousand guilders?"
"One? fifty thousand!" – was the exclamation
Of the astonished Mayor and Corporation.

Into the street the Piper stept,
    Smiling first a little smile,
As if he knew what magic slept
    In his quiet pipe the while;
Then, like a musical adept,
To blow the pipe his lips he wrinkled,
And green and blue his sharp eyes twinkled,
Like a candle-flame where salt is sprinkled;
And ere three shrill notes the pipe uttered,
You heard as if an army muttered;
And the muttering grew to a grumbling;
And the grumbling grew to a mighty rumbling;
And out of the houses the rats came tumbling.

Great rats, small rats, lean rats, brawny rats,
Brown rats, black rats, grey rats, tawny rats,
Grave old plodders, gay young friskers,
　　Fathers, mothers, uncles, cousins,
Cocking tails and pricking whiskers,
　　Families by tens and dozens,
Brothers, sisters, husbands, wives–
Followed the Piper for their lives.
From street to street he piped advancing,
And step for step they followed dancing,
Until they came to the river Weser,
　　Wherein all plunged and perished!
–Save one who, stout as Julius Caesar,
Swam across and lived to carry
　　(As he, the manuscript he cherished)
To Rat-land home his commentary:
Which was, "At the first shrill notes of the pipe,
I heard a sound as of scraping tripe,
And putting apples, wondrous ripe,
Into a cider-press's gripe:
And a moving away of pickle-tub-boards,
And a leaving ajar of conserve-cupboards,
And a drawing the corks of train-oil-flasks,
And a breaking the hoops of butter-casks;
And it seemed as if a voice
　　(Sweeter far than by harp or by psaltery
Is breathed) called out, 'Oh rats, rejoice!
　　The world is grown to one vast drysaltery!
So munch on, crunch on, take your nuncheon,
Breakfast, supper, dinner, luncheon!'
And just as a bulky sugar-puncheon,
All ready staved, like a great sun shone
Glorious scarce an inch before me,
Just as methought it said, 'Come, bore me!'
–I found the Weser rolling o'er me."

You should have heard the Hamelin people
Ringing the bells till they rocked the steeple.
"Go," cried the Mayor, "and get long poles,
Poke out the nests and block up the holes!
Consult with carpenters and builders,
And leave in our town not even a trace
Of the rats!" – when suddenly, up the face
Of the Piper perked in the market-place,
With a "First, if you please, my thousand guilders!"

A thousand guilders! The Mayor looked blue;
So did the Corporation too.
For council dinners made rare havoc
With Claret, Moselle, Vin-de-Grave, Hock;
And half the money would replenish
Their cellar's biggest butt with Rhenish.
To pay this sum to a wandering fellow
With a gipsy coat of red and yellow!
"Beside," quoth the Mayor with a knowing wink,
"Our business was done at the river's brink;
We saw with our eyes the vermin sink,
And what's dead can't come to life, I think.
So, friend, we're not the folks to shrink
From the duty of giving you something for drink,
And a matter of money to put in your poke;
But as for the guilders, what we spoke
Of them, as you very well know, was in joke.
Besides, our losses have made us thrifty.
A thousand guilders! Come, take fifty!"

The Piper's face fell, and he cried
"No trifling! I can't wait, beside!
I've promised to visit by dinnertime
Baghdad, and accept the prime
Of the Head-Cook's pottage, all he's rich in,
For having left, in the Caliph's kitchen,
Of a nest of scorpions no survivor:
With him I proved no bargain-driver,
With you, don't think I'll bate a stiver!
And folks who put me in a passion
May find me pipe after another fashion."

"How?" cried the Mayor, "d'ye think I brook
Being worse treated than a cook?
Insulted by a lazy ribald
With idle pipe and vesture piebald?
You threaten us, fellow? Do your worst,
Blow your pipe there till you burst!"

Once more he stepped into the street
    And to his lips again
    Laid his long pipe of smooth straight cane;
And ere he blew three notes (such sweet
Soft notes as yet musician's cunning
    Never gave the enraptured air)
There was a rustling that seemed like a bustling
Of merry crowds justling at pitching and hustling
Small feet were pattering, wooden shoes clattering,
Little hands clapping and little tongues chattering,
And, like fowls in a farmyard when barley is scattering,
Out came the children running.
All the little boys and girls,
With rosy cheeks and flaxen curls,
And sparkling eyes and teeth like pearls,
Tripping and skipping, ran merrily after
The wonderful music with shouting and laughter.

The Mayor was dumb, and the Council stood
As if they were changed into blocks of wood,
Unable to move a step, or cry
To the children merrily skipping by
—Could only follow with the eye
That joyous crowd at the Piper's back.
But how the Mayor was on the rack,
And the wretched Council's bosoms beat,
As the Piper turned from the High Street
To where the Weser rolled its waters
Right in the way of their sons and daughters!
However he turned from south to west,
And to Koppelberg Hill his steps addressed,
And after him the children pressed;
Great was the joy in every breast.
"He never can cross that mighty top!
He's forced to let the piping drop,
And we shall see our children stop!"
When, lo, as they reached the mountain-side,
A wondrous portal opened wide,
As if a cavern was suddenly hollowed;
And the Piper advanced and the children followed,
And when all were in to the very last,
The door in the mountain-side shut fast.
Did I say, all? No! One was lame,
    And could not dance the whole of the way;
And in after years, if you would blame
    His sadness, he was used to say–

"It's dull in our town since my playmates left!
I can't forget that I'm bereft
Of all the pleasant sights they see,
Which the Piper also promised me.
For he led us, he said, to a joyous land,
Joining the town and just at hand,
Where waters gushed and fruit trees grew
And flowers put forth a fairer hue,
And everything was strange and new;
The sparrows were brighter than peacocks here,
And their dogs outran our fallow deer,
And honey-bees had lost their stings,
And horses were born with eagles' wings:
And just as I became assured
My lame foot would be speedily cured,
The music stopped and I stood still,
And found myself outside the hill,
Left alone against my will,
To go now limping as before,
And never hear of that country more!"

Alas, alas for Hamelin!
    There came into many a burgher's pate
    A text which says that heaven's gate
    Opes to the rich at as easy rate
As the needle's eye takes a camel in!
The Mayor sent east, west, north and south,
To offer the Piper, by word of mouth,
    Wherever it was men's lot to find him,
Silver and gold to his heart's content,
If he'd only return the way he went,
    And bring the children behind him.

But when they saw 'twas a lost endeavour,
And Piper and dancers were gone for ever,
They made a decree that lawyers never
    Should think their records dated duly
If, after the day of the month and year,
These words did not as well appear,
"And so long after what happened here
    On the Twenty-second of July,
Thirteen hundred and seventy-six":
And the better in memory to fix
The place of the children's last retreat,
They called it the Pied Piper's Street—
Where anyone playing on pipe or tabor
Was sure for the future to lose his labour.
Nor suffered they hostelry or tavern
    To shock with mirth a street so solemn;
But opposite the place of the cavern
    They wrote the story on a column;

And on the great church-window painted
The same, to make the world acquainted
How their children were stolen away,
And there it stands to this very day.
And I must not omit to say
That in Transylvania there's a tribe
Of alien people who ascribe
The outlandish ways and dress
On which their neighbours lay such stress,
To their fathers and mothers having risen
Out of some subterraneous prison
Into which they were trepanned
Long time ago in a mighty band
Out of Hamelin town in Brunswick land,
But how or why, they don't understand.

So, Willy, let you and me be wipers
Of scores out with all men – especially pipers!
And, whether they pipe us free from rats or from mice,
If we've promised them aught, let us keep our promise!

ROBERT BROWNING

Ariel's Song

From "The Tempest"

Full fathom five thy father lies;
    Of his bones are coral made;
Those are pearls that were his eyes:
    Nothing of him that doth fade,
But doth suffer a sea-change
Into something rich and strange:
Sea nymphs hourly ring his knell.
        Ding-dong!
Hark! now I hear them,
        Ding-dong, bell!

WILLIAM SHAKESPEARE

The Snowman

Mother, while you were at the shops
and I was snoozing in my chair
I heard a tap at the window
saw a snowman standing there

He looked so cold and miserable
I almost could have cried
so I put the kettle on
and invited him inside

I made him a cup of cocoa
to warm the cockles of his nose
then he snuggled in front of the fire
for a cosy little doze

He lay there warm and smiling
softly counting sheep
I eavesdropped for a little while
then I too fell asleep

Seems he awoke and tiptoed out
exactly when I'm not too sure
it's a wonder you didn't see him
as you came in through the door

(oh, and by the way,
the kitten's made a puddle on the floor)

ROGER MCGOUGH

When All the World Is Full of Snow

I never know
just where to go,
when all the world
is full of snow.

I do not want
to make a track,
not even
to the shed and back.

I only want
to watch and wait,
while snow moths settle
on the gate,

and swarming frost flakes
fill the trees
with billions
of albino bees.

I only want
myself to be
as silent as
a winter tree,

to hear the swirling
stillness grow,
when all the world
is full of snow.

N.M. BODECKER

Encounter

We were sitting about taking coffee
in the aerodrome café at Copenhagen
where everything was brilliance and comfort
and stylish to the point of tedium.
The old man suddenly appeared
or rather happened like an event of nature,
in an ordinary greenish anorak
his face scarred by the salt and burning wind,
ploughing a furrow through the crowded room
and walking like a sailor from the wheel.
His beard was like the white foam of the sea
brimming and glistening around his face.
His gruffness and his winner's certainty
sent up a wave around him as he walked
through the old fashions aping modern fashions
and modern fashions aping old fashions.
He in his open collar and rough shirt
stepping aside from vermouth and pernod
stood at the bar demanding Russian vodka
and waving away soda with a "No".
He with the scars marking his tanned forearms
his filthy trousers and his noisy shoes
had better style than anyone in the crowd.
The solid ground seemed to quiver under
the heavy authority of that tread.
Somebody smiled across: "Look at that!
you'd think that was Hemingway," he said.
Expressed in details of his short gestures
and heavy motions of his fisherman's walk.

He was a statue sketched in a rough rock,
one treading down bullets and centuries,
one walking like a man hunched in a trench,
pushing aside people and furniture.
It was the very image of Hemingway.
(Later I heard that it was Hemingway.)

YEVGENY YEFTUSHENKO

The Soldier

If I should die, think only this of me:
    That there's some corner of a foreign field
That is for ever England. There shall be
    In that rich earth a richer dust concealed;
A dust whom England bore, shaped, made aware,
    Gave, once, her flowers to love, her ways to roam,
A body of England's, breathing English air,
    Washed by the rivers, blest by suns of home.

And think, this heart, all evil shed away,
    A pulse in the eternal mind, no less
        Gives somewhere back the thoughts by England
            given;
Her sights and sounds; dreams happy as her day;
    And laughter, learnt of friends; and gentleness,
        In hearts at peace, under an English heaven.

RUPERT BROOKE

45

Herbaceous Plodd

Herbaceous Plodd
is rather odd.
His eyes are red,
his nose is blue,
his neck and head
are joined by glue.
He only dines
on unripe peas,
bacon rinds
and melted cheese.
He rarely talks,
he never smiles,
but goes for walks
with crocodiles.

MICHAEL DUGAN

Mr Nobody

I know a funny little man,
    As quiet as a mouse,
Who does the mischief that is done
    In everybody's house!
There's no one ever sees his face,
    And yet we all agree
That every plate we break was cracked
    By Mr Nobody.

'Tis he who always tears our books,
    Who leaves the door ajar,
He pulls the buttons from our shirts,
    And scatters pins afar;
That squeaking door will always squeak
    For, prithee, don't you see,
We leave the oiling to be done
    By Mr Nobody.

He puts damp wood upon the fire,
    That kettles cannot boil;
His are the feet that bring in mud,
    And all the carpets soil.
The papers always are mislaid,
    Who had them last but he?
There's not one tosses them about
    But Mr Nobody.

The finger-marks upon the door
    By none of us are made;
We never leave the blinds unclosed,
    To let the curtains fade;
The ink we never spill; the boots
    That lying round you see
Are not our boots; they all belong
    To Mr Nobody.

UNKNOWN

47

Sing a Song of People

Sing a song of people
    Walking fast or slow;
People in the city,
    Up and down they go.

    People on the sidewalk,
    People on the bus;
    People passing, passing,
    In back and front of us.
    People on the subway
    Underneath the ground;
    People riding taxis
    Round and round and round.

Some People

Isn't it strange some people make
    You feel so tired inside,
Your thoughts begin to shrivel up
    Like leaves all brown and dried!

But when you're with some other ones,
    It's stranger still to find
Your thoughts as thick as fireflies
    All shiny in your mind!

RACHEL FIELD

People with their hats on,
Going in the doors;
People with umbrellas
When it rains and pours.
People in tall buildings
And in stores below;
Riding elevators
Up and down they go.

People walking singly,
People in a crowd;
People saying nothing,
People talking loud.
People laughing, smiling,
Grumpy people too;
People who just hurry
And never look at you!

Sing a song of people
    Who like to come and go;
Sing of city people
    You see but never know!

LOIS LENSKI

SEASONS AND CELEBRATIONS

there's all sorts of rhyme and seasonal weather
together in this section
but you won't need your wellies
or umbrellies
for protection

Pancakes

Mix a pancake,
Stir a pancake,
   Pop it in the pan;
Fry the pancake,
Toss the pancake,–
   Catch it if you can.

CHRISTINA ROSSETTI

It's Never Fair Weather

I do not like the winter wind
That whistles from the North.
My upper teeth and those beneath
They jitter back and forth.
Oh, some are hanged, and some are skinned,
And others face the winter wind.

      I do not like the summer sun
      That scorches the horizon.
      Though some delight in Fahrenheit,
      To me it's deadly pizen.
      I think that life would be more fun
      Without the simmering summer sun.

            I do not like the signs of spring,
            The fever and the chills,
            The icy mud, the puny bud,
            The frozen daffodils.
            Let other poets gaily sing;
            I do not like the signs of spring.

I do not like the foggy fall
That strips the maples bare;
The radiator's mating call,
The dank, rheumatic air;
I fear that taken all in all,
I do not like the foggy fall.

The winter sun, of course, is kind,
And summer's wind a saviour,
And I'll merrily sing of fall and spring
When they're on their good behaviour.
But otherwise I see no reason
To speak in praise of any season.

OGDEN NASH

The first of April

The first of April, some do say,
Is set apart for All Fools' Day,
But why the people call it so
Nor I nor they themselves do know.

UNKNOWN

Celebration

I don't like weddings, not at all,
I find them just a bore,
At least, that's how it's always seemed,
When I've been to them before.
There's all those *boring* relatives,
That come from far and near,
Scoffing little triangular sandwiches,
And swigging wine and pints of beer,
Saying, "Don't the bridesmaids all look sweet?"
And, "Isn't it a pity,
That the best man's wearing two odd socks?"
Or "Was ever a bride so pretty?"
But I can't wait for Saturday,
To see Aunt Beryl's face,
'Cos cousin Cheryl's marrying,
A Thing from Outer Space!

WILLIS HALL

Home Thoughts from Abroad

Oh, to be in England
Now that April's there,
And whoever wakes in England
Sees, some morning, unaware,
That the lowest boughs and the brushwood sheaf
Round the elm-tree bole are in tiny leaf,
While the chaffinch sings on the orchard bough
In England – now!

And after April, when May follows,
And the whitethroat builds, and all the swallows!
Hark, where my blossomed pear-tree in the hedge
Leans to the field and scatters on the clover
Blossoms and dewdrops – at the bent spray's edge–
That's the wise thrush; he sings each song twice over,
Lest you should think he never could recapture
The first fine careless rapture!
And though the fields look rough with hoary dew
All will be gay when noontide wakes anew
The buttercups, the little children's dower
–Far brighter than this gaudy melon-flower!

ROBERT BROWNING

Weathers

This is the weather the cuckoo likes,
    And so do I;
When showers betumble the chestnut spikes,
    And nestlings fly:
And the little brown nightingale bills his best,
And they sit outside at "The Traveller's Rest",
And maids come forth sprig-muslin drest,
And citizens dream of the south and west,
    And so do I.

This is the weather the shepherd shuns,
    And so do I;
When beeches drip in brown and duns,
    And thresh, and ply;
And hill-hid tides throb, throe on throe,
And meadow rivulets overflow,
And drops on gate-bars hang in a row,
And rooks in families homeward go,
    And so do I.

THOMAS HARDY

Adlestrop

Yes. I remember Adlestrop –
The name, because one afternoon
Of heat the express-train drew up there
Unwontedly. It was late June.

The steam hissed. Someone cleared his throat.
No one left and no one came
On the bare platform. What I saw
Was Adlestrop – only the name

And willows, willow-herb, and grass,
And meadowsweet, and haycocks dry,
No whit less still and lonely fair
Than the high cloudlets in the sky.

And for that minute a blackbird sang
Close by, and round him, mistier,
Farther and farther, all the birds
Of Oxfordshire and Gloucestershire.

EDWARD THOMAS

Under the Greenwood Tree

from "As You Like It"

Under the greenwood tree
Who loves to lie with me,
And turn his merry note
Unto the sweet bird's throat–
Come hither, come hither, come hither!
    Here shall he see
    No enemy
But winter and rough weather.

Who doth ambition shun
And loves to live i' th' sun,
Seeking the food he eats
And pleased with what he gets,
Come hither, come hither, come hither!
    Here shall he see
    No enemy
But winter and rough weather.

WILLIAM SHAKESPEARE

A Hot Day

Cottonwool clouds loiter.
A lawnmower, very far,
Birrs. Then a bee comes
To a crimson rose and softly,
Deftly and fatly crams
A velvet body in.

A tree, June-lazy, makes
A tent of dim green light.
Sunlight weaves in the leaves,
Honey-light laced with leaf-light,
Green interleaved with gold.
Sunlight gathers its rays
In sheaves, which the wind unweaves
And then reweaves – the wind
That puffs a smell of grass
Through the heat-heavy, trembling
Summer pool of air.

A. S. J. TESSIMOND

Ode To Autumn

Season of mists and mellow fruitfulness!
    Close bosom-friend of the maturing sun;
Conspiring with him how to load and bless
    With fruit the vines that round the thatch-eaves run;
To bend with apples the moss'd cottage-trees,
    And fill all fruit with ripeness to the core;
      To swell the gourd, and plump the hazel shells
    With a sweet kernel; to set budding more,
And still more, later flowers for the bees,
Until they think warm days will never cease,
      For Summer has o'er-brimm'd their clammy cells.

Who hath not seen thee oft amid thy store?
    Sometimes whoever seeks abroad may find
Thee sitting careless on a granary floor,
    Thy hair soft-lifted by the winnowing wind;
Or on a half-reap'd furrow sound asleep,
    Drowsed with the fumes of poppies, while thy hook
      Spares the next swath and all its twinèd flowers;
And sometimes like a gleaner thou dost keep
    Steady thy laden head across a brook;
    Or by a cider-press, with patient look,
      Thou watchest the last oozings, hours by hours.

Where are the songs of Spring? Ay, where are they?
   Think not of them, thou hast thy music too,
     While barred clouds bloom the soft-dying day,
And touch the stubble-plains with rosy hue;
   Then in a wailful choir the small gnats mourn
   Among the river sallows, borne aloft
     Or sinking as the light wind lives or dies;
And full-grown lambs loud bleat from hilly bourn;
   Hedge-crickets sing; and now with treble soft
   The redbreast whistles from a garden-croft,
     And gathering swallows twitter in the skies.

JOHN KEATS

Just Another Autumn Day

In Parliament, the Minister for Mists
and Mellow Fruitfulness announces,
that owing to inflation and rising costs
there will be no Autumn next year.
September, October and November
are to be cancelled,
and the Government to bring in
the nine-month year instead.
Thus will we all live longer.

Emergency measures are to be introduced
to combat outbreaks of well-being
and feelings of elation inspired by the season.
Breathtaking sunsets will be restricted
to alternate Fridays, and gentle dusks
prohibited. Fallen leaves will be outlawed,
and persons found in possession of conkers,
imprisoned without trial.
Thus will we all work harder.

The announcement caused little reaction.
People either way don't really care
No time have they to stand and stare
Looking for work or slaving away
Just another Autumn day.

ROGER MCGOUGH

Apple-Time

Your time is come, you apple-trees,
 Your labours weigh upon the bough,
Your heavy branches ask for ease
 And here we come to ease them now.
In April's hour of bridal bliss
You bloomed for this, you bloomed for this.

All day the lengthy ladders lean
 Their stairs against the twisty trunk;
We mount on them to chambers green,
 And before twilight falls are drunk
As bees upon the heady scent
In which the golden day was spent.

The baskets bear away the yield:
 Dull Russet, glossy Quarrenden,
Green Wellington, and scarlet-peeled
 Pearmain; the arms of girls and men
Ache with the streaked and yellow bales
Of Pippins and small Curlytails.

And some must to the cider-press
 Their juices in the crush to spill,
Some to the larder, some to dress
 The table, some must barrels fill,
And some must to the apple-loft
Whence greedy hands shall steal them oft.

The ruddy apple of the sun,
 The golden apple of the night,
Shall watch our toil till all is done,
 And we grow tired as you grow light.
You apple-trees, give up your sun,
Your time is come, your time is come.

ELEANOR FARJEON

Stopping by Woods on a Snowy Evening

Whose woods these are I think I know.
His house is in the village though;
He will not see me stopping here
To watch his woods fill up with snow.

My little horse must think it queer
To stop without a farmhouse near
Between the woods and frozen lake
The darkest evening of the year.

He gives his harness bells a shake
To ask if there is some mistake.
The only other sound's the sweep
Of easy wind and downy flake.

The woods are lovely, dark and deep,
But I have promises to keep,
And miles to go before I sleep,
And miles to go before I sleep.

ROBERT FROST

The Old Year

The Old Year's gone away
    To nothingness and night:
We cannot find him all the day
    Nor hear him in the night:
He left no footstep, mark or place
    In either shade or sun:
The last year he'd a neighbour's face,
    In this he's known by none.

All nothing everywhere:
    Mists we on mornings see
Have more of substance when they're here
    And more of form than he.
He was a friend by every fire,
    In every cot and hall –
A guest to every heart's desire,
    And now he's nought at all.

Old papers thrown away,
    Old garments cast aside,
The talk of yesterday,
    All things identified;
But times once torn away
    No voices can recall:
The eve of New Year's Day
    Left the Old Year lost to all.

JOHN CLARE

TIMES PAST

you can use this book
if you want to look
at the ways and days that have been
and while you do
if you want to
you can pretend that you're in a time machine

The Lady of Shalott

Part 1

On either side the river lie
Long fields of barley and of rye,
That clothe the wold and meet the sky;
And thro' the field the road runs by
　　　To many-tower'd Camelot;
And up and down the people go,
Gazing where the lilies blow
Round an island there below,
　　　The island of Shalott.

Willows whiten, aspens quiver,
Little breezes dusk and shiver
Thro' the wave that runs for ever
By the island in the river
　　　Flowing down to Camelot.
Four gray walls, and four gray towers,
Overlook a space of flowers,
And the silent isle imbowers
　　　The Lady of Shalott.

By the margin, willow-veil'd,
Slide the heavy barges trail'd
By slow horses; and unhail'd
The shallop flitteth silken-sail'd
　　　Skimming down to Camelot:
But who hath seen her wave her hand?
Or at the casement seen her stand?
Or is she known in all the land,
　　　The Lady of Shalott?

Only reapers, reaping early
In among the bearded barley,
Hear a song that echoes cheerly
From the river winding clearly,
　　　Down to tower'd Camelot:
And by the moon the reaper weary,
Piling sheaves in uplands airy,
Listening, whispers "Tis the fairy
　　　Lady of Shalott."

And moving thro' a mirror clear
That hangs before her all the year,
Shadows of the world appear.
There she sees the highway near
      Winding down to Camelot:
There the river eddy whirls,
And there the surly village-churls,
And the red cloaks of market girls,
      Pass onward from Shalott.

Sometimes a troop of damsels glad,
An abbot on an ambling pad,
Sometimes a curly shepherd-lad,
Or long-hair'd page in crimson clad,
      Goes by to tower'd Camelot;
And sometimes thro' the mirror blue
The knights come riding two and two:
She hath no loyal knight and true,
      The Lady of Shalott.

Part 2

There she weaves by night and day
A magic web with colours gay.
She has heard a whisper say,
A curse is on her if she stay
      To look down to Camelot.
She knows not what the curse may be,
And so she weaveth steadily,
And little other care hath she,
      The Lady of Shalott.

But in her web she still delights
To weave the mirror's magic sights,
For often thro' the silent nights,
A funeral, with plumes and lights
      And music, went to Camelot:
Or when the moon was overhead,
Came two young lovers lately wed;
"I am half sick of shadows," said
      The Lady of Shalott.

Part 3

A bow-shot from her bower-eaves,
He rode between the barley-sheaves,
The sun came dazzling thro' the leaves,
And flamed upon the brazen greaves
    Of bold Sir Lancelot.
A red-cross knight for ever kneel'd
To a lady in his shield,
That sparkled on the yellow field,
    Beside remote Shalott.

The gemmy bridle glitter'd free,
Like to some branch of stars we see
Hung in the golden Galaxy.
The bridle bells rang merrily
    As he rode down to Camelot:
And from his blazon'd baldric slung
A mighty silver bugle hung,
And as he rode his armour rung,
    Beside remote Shalott.

All in the blue unclouded weather
Thick-jewell'd shone the saddle-leather,
The helmet and the helmet-feather
Burn'd like one burning flame together,
    As he rode down to Camelot.
As often thro' the purple night,
Below the starry clusters bright,
Some bearded meteor, trailing light,
    Moves over still Shalott.

His broad clear brow in sunlight glow'd;
On burnish'd hooves his war-horse trode;
From underneath his helmet flow'd
His coal-black curls as on he rode,
    As he rode down to Camelot.
From the bank and from the river
He flash'd into the crystal mirror,
"Tirra lirra," by the river
    Sang Sir Lancelot.

She left the web, she left the loom,
She made three paces thro' the room,
She saw the water-lily bloom,
She saw the helmet and the plume,
    She look'd down to Camelot.
Out flew the web and floated wide;
The mirror crack'd from side to side;
"The curse is come upon me," cried
    The Lady of Shalott.

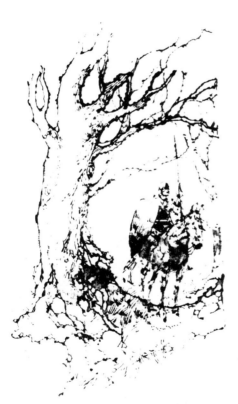

Part 4

In the stormy east-wind straining,
The pale yellow woods were waning,
The broad stream in his banks complaining,
Heavily the low sky raining
     Over tower'd Camelot;
Down she came and found a boat
Beneath a willow left afloat,
And round about the prow she wrote
     The Lady of Shalott.

And down the river's dim expanse
Like some bold seër in a trance,
Seeing all his own mischance –
With a glassy countenance
     Did she look to Camelot.
And at the closing of the day
She loosed the chain, and down she lay;
The broad stream bore her far away,
     The Lady of Shalott.

Lying, robed in snowy white
That loosely flew to left and right –
The leaves upon her falling light –
Thro' the noises of the night
     She floated down to Camelot:
And as the boat-head wound along
The willowy hills and fields among,
They heard her singing her last song,
     The Lady of Shalott.

Heard a carol, mournful, holy,
Chanted loudly, chanted lowly,
Till her blood was frozen slowly,
And her eyes were darken'd wholly,
     Turn'd to tower'd Camelot.
For ere she reach'd upon the tide
The first house by the water-side,
Singing in her song she died,
     The Lady of Shalott.

Under tower and balcony,
By garden-wall and gallery,
A gleaming shape she floated by,
Dead-pale between the houses high,
     Silent into Camelot.
Out upon the wharfs they came,
Knight and burgher, lord and dame,
And round the prow they read her name,
     The Lady of Shalott.

Who is this? and what is here?
And in the lighted palace near
Died the sound of royal cheer;
And they cross'd themselves for fear,
     All the knights at Camelot:
But Lancelot mused a little space;
He said, "She has a lovely face;
God in his mercy lend her grace,
     The Lady of Shalott."

ALFRED,
LORD TENNYSON

73

Kubla Khan

In Xanadu did Kubla Khan
    A stately pleasure-dome decree:
Where Alph, the sacred river, ran
Through caverns measureless to man
    Down to a sunless sea.
So twice five miles of fertile ground
    With walls and towers were girdled round:
And there were gardens bright with sinuous rills
Where blossomed many an incense-bearing tree;
And here were forests ancient as the hills,
Enfolding sunny spots of greenery.

But O, that deep romantic chasm which slanted
Down the green hill athwart a cedarn cover!
A savage place! as holy and enchanted
As e'er beneath a waning moon was haunted
By woman wailing for her demon-lover!
And from this chasm, with ceaseless turmoil seething,
As if this earth in fast thick pants were breathing,
A mighty fountain momently was forced;
Amid whose swift half-intermitted burst
Huge fragments vaulted like rebounding hail,
Or chaffy grain beneath the thresher's flail:
And 'mid these dancing rocks at once and ever
It flung up momently the sacred river.
Five miles meandering with a mazy motion
Through wood and dale the sacred river ran,
Then reached the caverns measureless to man,
And sank in tumult to a lifeless ocean:
And 'mid this tumult Kubla heard from far
Ancestral voices prophesying war!

The shadow of the dome of pleasure
    Floated midway on the waves;
Where was heard the mingled measure
    From the fountain and the caves.
It was a miracle of rare device,
A sunny pleasure-dome with caves of ice!

A damsel with a dulcimer
    In a vision once I saw:
It was an Abyssinian maid,
    And on her dulcimer she played,
Singing of Mount Abora.
Could I revive within me,
    Her symphony and song,
To such a deep delight 'twould win me,
That with music loud and long,
I would build that dome in air,
That sunny dome! those caves of ice!
And all who heard should see them there,
And all should cry, Beware! Beware!
His flashing eyes, his floating hair!
Weave a circle round him thrice,
    And close your eyes with holy dread,
    For he on honey-dew hath fed,
And drunk the milk of Paradise.

SAMUEL TAYLOR COLERIDGE

Ozymandias

I met a traveller from an antique land
Who said: Two vast and trunkless legs of stone
Stand in the desert...Near them, on the sand,
Half sunk, a shattered visage lies, whose frown,
And wrinkled lip, and sneer of cold command,
Tell that its sculptor well those passions read
Which yet survive, stamped on these lifeless things,
The hand that mocked them, and the heart that fed:
And on the pedestal these words appear:
"My name is Ozymandias, king of kings:
Look on my works, ye Mighty, and despair!"
Nothing beside remains. Round the decay
Of that colossal wreck, boundless and bare
The lone and level sands stretch far away.

PERCY BYSSHE SHELLEY

Eldorado

Gaily bedight,
A gallant knight
In sunshine and in shadow,
Had journeyed long,
Singing a song,
In search of Eldorado.

But he grew old –
This knight so bold –
And o'er his heart a shadow
Fell, as he found
No spot of ground
That looked like Eldorado.

And as his strength
Failed him at length,
He met a pilgrim shadow:
"Shadow," said he,
"Where can it be,
This land of Eldorado?"

"Over the mountains
Of the Moon,
Down the valley of Shadow,
Ride, boldly ride,"
The shade replied,
"If you seek for Eldorado."

EDGAR ALLEN POE

From

The Song of Hiawatha

Out of childhood into manhood
Now had grown my Hiawatha,
Skilled in all the craft of hunters,
Learned in all the lore of old men,
In all youthful sports and pastimes,
In all manly arts and labours.

    Swift of foot was Hiawatha;
He could shoot an arrow from him,
And run forward with such fleetness,
That the arrow fell behind him!
Strong of arm was Hiawatha;
He could shoot ten arrows upward,
Shoot them with such strength and
    swiftness,
That the tenth had left the bow-
    string
Ere the first to earth had fallen!

    He had mittens, Minjekahwun,
Magic mittens made of deerskin;
When upon his hands he wore them,
He could smite the rocks asunder,
He could grind them into powder.
He had moccasins enchanted,
Magic moccasins of deerskin;
When he bound them round his
    ankles,
When upon his feet he tied them,
At each stride a mile he measured!

    Much he questioned old Nokomis
Of his father Mudjekeewis;
Learned from her the fatal secret
Of the beauty of his mother,

Of the falsehood of his father;
And his heart was hot within him,
Like a living coal his heart was.

    Then he said to old Nokomis,
"I will go to Mudjekeewis,
See how fares it with my father,
At the doorways of the West-
    Wind,
At the portals of the Sunset!"

    From his lodge went Hiawatha,
Dressed for travel, armed for hunt-
    ing;
Dressed in deerskin shirt and
    leggings,
Richly wrought with quills and
    wampum;
On his head his eagle-feathers,
Round his waist his belt on
    wampum,
In his hand his bow of ash-wood,
Strung with sinews of the reindeer;
In his quiver oaken arrows,
Tipped with jasper, winged with
    feathers;
With his mittens, Minjekahwun,
With his moccasins enchanted.

    Warning said the old Nokomis,
"Go not forth, O Hiawatha!
To the kingdom of the West-Wind,
To the realms of Mudjekeewis,
Lest he harm you with his magic,
Lest he kill you with his cunning!"

But the fearless Hiawatha
Heeded not her woman's warning;
Forth he strode into the forest,
At each stride a mile he measured;
Lurid seemed the sky above him,
Lurid seemed the earth beneath him,
Hot and close the air around him,
Filled with smoke and fiery vapours,
As of burning woods and prairies,
For his heart was hot within him,
Like a living coal his heart was.

So he journeyed westward, west-
        ward,
Left the fleetest deer behind him,
Left the antelope and bison;
Crossed the rushing Esconaba,
Crossed the mighty Mississippi,
Passed the Mountains of the Prairie,
Passed the land of Crows and
        Foxes,
Passed the dwellings of the Black-
        feet,
Came unto the Rocky Mountains,
To the kingdom of the West-Wind,
Where upon the gusty summits
Sat the ancient Mudjekeewis,
Ruler of the winds of heaven.

Filled with awe was Hiawatha
At the aspect of his father.
On the air about him wildly
Tossed and streamed his cloudy
        tresses,
Gleamed like drifting snow his
        tresses,
Glared like Ishkoodah, the comet,
Like the star with fiery tresses.

Filled with joy was Mudjekeewis
When he looked on Hiawatha,
Saw his youth rise up before him
In the face of Hiawatha,
Saw the beauty of Wenonah
From the grave rise up before him.

"Welcome!" said he, "Hiawatha,
To the kingdom of the West-Wind!
Long have I been waiting for you!
Youth is lovely, age is lonely,
Youth is fiery, age is frosty;
You bring back the days departed,
You bring back my youth of
        passion,
And the beautiful Wenonah!"

Many days they talked together,
Questioned, listened, waited, an-
        swered;
Much the mighty Mudjekeewis
Boasted of his ancient prowess,
Of his perilous adventures,
His indomitable courage,
His invulnerable body.

Patiently sat Hiawatha,
Listening to his father's boasting;
With a smile he sat and listened,
Uttered neither threat nor menace,
Neither word nor look betrayed him;
But his heart was hot within him,
Like a living coal his heart was.

Then he said, "O Mudjekeewis,
Is there nothing that can harm you?
Nothing that you are afraid of?"
And the mighty Mudjekeewis,
Grand and gracious in his boasting,
Answered, saying, "There is no-
        thing,

Nothing but the black rock yonder,
Nothing but the fatal Wawbeek!"
    And he looked at Hiawatha
With a wise look and benignant,
With a countenance paternal,
Looked with pride upon the beauty
Of his tall and graceful figure,
Saying, "O my Hiawatha!
Is there anything can harm you?
Anything you are afraid of?"
    But the wary Hiawatha
Paused awhile, as if uncertain,
Held his peace, as if resolving,
And then answered, "There is no-
        thing,
Nothing but the bulrush yonder,
Nothing but the great Apukwa!"
    And as Mudjekeewis, rising,
Stretched his hand to pluck the
        bulrush,
Hiawatha cried in terror,
Cried in well-dissembled terror,
"Kago! kago! do not touch it!"
"Ah, kaween!" said Mudjekeewis,
"No indeed, I will not touch it!"
    Then they talked of other
        matters;
First of Hiawatha's brothers,
First of Wabun, of the East-Wind,
Of the South-Wind, Shawondasee,
Of the North, Kabibonokka;
Then of Hiawatha's mother,
Of the beautiful Wenonah,
Of her birth upon the meadow,
Of her death, as old Nokomis
Had remembered and related.

    And he cried, "O Mudjekeewis,
It was you who killed Wenonah,
Took her young life and her beauty,
Broke the Lily of the Prairie,
Trampled it beneath your footsteps;
You confess it! you confess it!"
And the mighty Mudjekeewis
Tossed upon the wind his tresses,
Bowed his hoary head in anguish,
With a silent nod assented.
    Then upstarted Hiawatha,
And with threatening look and
        gesture
Laid his hand upon the black rock,
On the fatal Wawbeek laid it,
With his mittens, Minjekahwun,
Rent the jutting crag asunder,
Smote and crushed it into frag-
        ments,
Hurled them madly at his father,
The remorseful Mudjekeewis;
For his heart was hot within him,
Like a living coal his heart was.
    But the ruler of the West-Wind
Blew the fragments backward from
        him,
With the breathing of his nostrils,
With the tempest of his anger,
Blew them back at his assailant;
Seized the bulrush, the Apukwa,
Dragged it with its roots and fibres
From the margin of the meadow,
From its ooze, the giant bulrush;
Long and loud laughed Hiawatha!
    Then began the deadly conflict,
Hand to hand among the moun-
        tains;

From his eyrie screamed the eagle,
The Keneu, the great war-eagle;
Sat upon the crags around them,
Wheeling flapped his wings above
them.
Like a tall tree in the tempest
Bent and lashed the giant bulrush;
And in masses huge and heavy
Crashing fell the fatal Wawbeek;
Till the earth shook with the
tumult
And confusion of the battle,
And the air was full of shoutings,
And the thunder of the mountains,
Starting, answered, "Baim-wawa!"
Back retreated Mudjekeewis,
Rushing westward o'er the moun-
tains,
Stumbling westward down the
mountains,
Three whole days retreated fighting,
Still pursued by Hiawatha
To the doorways of the West-Wind,
To the portals of the Sunset,
To the earth's remotest border,
Where into the empty spaces
Sinks the sun, as a flamingo
Drops into her nest at nightfall,
In the melancholy marshes.
"Hold!" at length cried Mud-
jekeewis,
"Hold, my son, my Hiawatha!
'Tis impossible to kill me,
For you cannot kill the immortal
I have put you to this trial,
But to know and prove your courage;
Now receive the prize of valour!

Go back to your home and
people,
Live among them, toil among them,
Cleanse the earth from all that
harms it,
Clear the fishing-grounds and
rivers,
Slay all monsters and magicians,
All the Wendigoes, the giants,
All the serpents, the Kenabeeks,
As I slew the Mishe-Mokwa,
Slew the Great Bear of the moun-
tains.
And at last when Death draws
near you,
When the awful eyes of Pauguk
Glare upon you in the darkness,
I will share my kingdom with you;
Ruler shall you be thenceforward
Of the Northwest-Wind, Keeway-
din,
Of the home-wind, the Keewaydin."
Thus was fought that famous
battle
In the dreadful days of Shah-shah,
In the days long since departed,
In the kingdom of the West-Wind.
Still the hunter sees its traces
Scattered far o'er hill and valley;
Sees the giant bulrush growing
By the ponds and water-courses,
Sees the masses of the Wawbeek
Lying still in every valley.
Homeward now went Hiawatha;
Pleasant was the landscape round
him,
Pleasant was the air above him,

For the bitterness of anger
Had departed wholly from him,
From his brain the thought of ven-
geance,
From his heart the burning fever.
  Only once his pace he slackened,
Only once he paused or halted,
Paused to purchase heads of arrows
Of the ancient Arrow-maker,
In the land of the Dacotahs,
Where the Falls of Minnehaha
Flash and gleam among the oak-
trees,
Laugh and leap into the valley.
  There the ancient Arrow-maker
Made his arrow-heads of sand-
stone,
Arrow-heads of chalcedony,
Arrow-heads of flint and jasper,
Smoothed and sharpened at the
edges,
Hard and polished, keen and
costly.
  With him dwelt his dark-eyed
daughter,
Wayward as the Minnehaha,
With her moods of shade and sun-
shine,
Eyes that smiled and frowned al-
ternate,
Feet as rapid as the river,
Tresses flowing like the water,

And as musical a laughter;
And he named her from the river,
From the waterfall he named her,
Minnehaha, Laughing Water.
  Was it then for heads of arrows,
Arrow-heads of chalcedony,
Arrow-heads of flint and jasper,
That my Hiawatha halted
In the land of the Dacotahs?
  Was it not to see the maiden,
See the face of Laughing Water
Peeping from behind the curtain,
Hear the rustling of her garments
From behind the waving curtain,
As one sees the Minnehaha
Gleaming, glancing through the
branches,
As one hears the Laughing Water
From behind its screen of branches?
  Who shall say what thoughts
and visions
Fill the fiery brains of young men?
Who shall say what dreams of
beauty
Filled the heart of Hiawatha?
All he told to old Nokomis,
When he reached the lodge at
sunset,
Was the meeting with his father,
Was his fight with Mudjekeewis;
Not a word he said of arrows,
Not a word of Laughing Water.

HENRY
LONGFELLOW

The Rolling English Road

Before the Roman came to Rye or out to Severn strode,
The rolling English drunkard made the rolling English road.
A reeling road, a rolling road, that rambles round the shire,
And after him the parson ran, the sexton and the squire;
A merry road, a mazy road, and such as we did tread
The night we went to Birmingham by way of Beachy Head.

I knew no harm of Bonaparte and plenty of the Squire,
And for to fight the Frenchman I did not much desire;
But I did bash their baggonets because they came arrayed
To straighten out the crooked road an English drunkard made,
Where you and I went down the lane with ale-mugs in our hands,
The night we went to Glastonbury by way of Goodwin Sands.

His sins they were forgiven him; or why do flowers run
Behind him; and the hedges all strengthening in the sun?
The wild thing went from left to right and knew not which was which,
But the wild rose was above him when they found him in the ditch.
God pardon us, nor harden us; we did not see so clear
The night we went to Bannockburn by way of Brighton Pier.

My friends, we will not go again or ape an ancient rage,
Or stretch the folly of our youth to be the shame of age,
But walk with clearer eyes and ears this path that wandereth,
And see undrugged in evening light the decent inn of death;
For there is good news yet to hear and fine things to be seen,
Before we go to Paradise by way of Kensal Green.

G. K. CHESTERTON

Italy versus England

With all its sinful doings, I must say,
    That Italy's a pleasant place to me,
Who love to see the sun shine every day,
    And vines (not nailed to walls) from tree to tree
Festooned, much like the back scene of a play,
    Or melodrame, which people flock to see,
When the first act is ended by a dance
In vineyards copied from the South of France.

I like on autumn evenings to ride out,
    Without being forced to bid my groom be sure
My cloak is round his middle strapped about,
    Because the skies are not the most secure;
I know too that, if stopped upon my route,
    Where the green alleys windingly allure,
Reeling with grapes red wagons choke the way.—
In England 'twould be dung, dust, or a dray.

I also like to dine on becaficas,
    To see the sun set, sure he'll rise to-morrow,
Not through a misty morning twinkling weak as
    A drunken man's dead eye in maudlin sorrow,
But with all Heaven to himself; the day will break as
    Beauteous as cloudless, nor be forced to borrow
That sort of farthing candlelight which glimmers
Where reeking London's smoky cauldron simmers.

I love the language, that soft bastard Latin,
    Which melts like kisses from a female mouth,
And sounds as if it should be writ on satin,
    With syllables which breathe of the sweet South,
And gentle liquids gliding all so pat in,
    That not a single accent seems uncouth,
Like our harsh northern whistling, grunting guttural,
Which we're obliged to hiss, and spit, and sputter all.

I like the women too (forgive my folly!),
    From the rich peasant cheek of ruddy bronze,
And large black eyes that flash on you a volley
    Of rays that say a thousand things at once,
To the high Dama's brow, more melancholy,
    But clear, and with a wild and liquid glance,
Heart on her lips, and soul within her eyes,
Soft as her clime, and sunny as her skies.

Eve of the land which still is Paradise!
    Italian Beauty! didst thou not inspire
Raphael, who died in thy embrace, and vies
    With all we know of Heaven, or can desire,
In what he hath bequeathed us? – in what guise,
    Though flashing from the fervour of the lyre,
Would *words* describe thy past and present glow,
While yet Canova can create below?

"England! with all thy faults I love thee still",
    I said at Calais, and have not forgot it;
I like to speak and lucubrate my fill;
    I like the government (but that is not it);
I like the freedom of the press and quill;
    I like the Habeas Corpus (when we've got it);
I like a Parliamentary debate,
Particularly when 'tis not too late;

I like the taxes, when they're not too many;
    I like a seacoal fire, when not too dear;
I like a beef-steak, too, as well as any;
    Have no objection to a pot of beer;
I like the weather, – when it is not rainy,
    That is, I like two months of every year.
And so God save the Regent, Church, and King!
Which means that I like all and every thing.

Our standing army, and disbanded seamen,
    Poor's rate, Reform, my own, the nation's debt,
Our little riots just to show we're free men,
    Our trifling bankruptcies in the Gazette,
Our cloudy climate, and our chilly women,
    All these I can forgive, and those forget,
And greatly venerate our recent glories,
And wish they were not owing to the Tories.

LORD BYRON

Morte d'Arthur

So all day long the noise of battle roll'd
Among the mountains by the winter sea;
Until King Arthur's table, man by man,
Had fallen in Lyonnesse about their Lord,
King Arthur: then, because his wound was deep,
The bold Sir Bedivere uplifted him,
Sir Bedivere, the last of all his knights,
And bore him to a chapel nigh the field,
A broken chancel with a broken cross,
That stood on a dark strait of barren land.
On one side lay the Ocean, and on one
Lay a great water, and the moon was full.
   Then spake King Arthur to Sir Bedivere:
"The sequel of to-day unsolders all

The goodliest fellowship of famous knights
Whereof this world holds record. Such a sleep
They sleep – the men I loved. I think that we
Shall never more, at any future time,
Delight our souls with talk of knightly deeds,
Walking about the gardens and the halls
Of Camelot, as in the days that were.
I perish by this people which I made,–
Tho' Merlin sware that I should come again
To rule once more – but let what will be, be,
I am so deeply smitten thro' the helm
That without help I cannot last till morn.
Thou therefore take my brand Excalibur,
Which was my pride: for thou rememberest how
In those old days, one summer noon, an arm
Rose up from out the bosom of the lake,
Clothed in white samite, mystic, wonderful,
Holding the sword – and how I row'd across
And took it, and have worn it, like a king:
And, wheresoever I am sung or told
In aftertime, this also shall be known:
But now delay not: take Excalibur,
And fling him far into the middle mere:
Watch what thou seëst, and lightly bring me word."
   To him replied the bold Sir Bedivere:
"It is not meet, Sir King, to leave thee thus,
Aidless, alone, and smitten thro' the helm.
A little thing may harm a wounded man.
Yet I thy hest will all perform at full,
Watch what I see, and lightly bring thee word."
   So saying, from the ruin'd shrine he stept
And in the moon athwart the place of tombs,
Where lay the mighty bones of ancient men,
Old knights, and over them the sea-wind sang
Shrill, chill, with flakes of foam. He, stepping down
By zig-zag paths, and juts of pointed rock,
Came on the shining levels of the lake.
   There drew he forth the brand Excalibur,
And o'er him, drawing it, the winter moon,
Brightening the skirts of a long cloud, ran forth
And sparkled keen with frost against the hilt:
For all the haft twinkled with diamond sparks,
Myriads of topaz-lights, and jacinth-work
Of subtlest jewellery. He gazed so long
That both his eyes were dazzled, as he stood,

This way and that dividing the swift mind,
In act to throw: but at the last it seem'd
Better to leave Excalibur conceal'd
There in the many-knotted waterflags,
That whistled stiff and dry about the marge.
So strode he back slow to the wounded King.
    Then spake King Arthur to Sir Bedivere:
"Hast thou perform'd my mission which I gave?
What is it thou hast seen? or what hast heard?"
    And answer made the bold Sir Bedivere:
"I heard the ripple washing in the reeds,
And the wild water lapping on the crag."
    To whom replied King Arthur, faint and pale:
"Thou hast betray'd thy nature and thy name,
Not rendering true answer, as beseem'd
Thy fëalty, nor like a noble knight:
For surer sign had follow'd, either hand,
Or voice, or else a motion of the mere.
This is a shameful thing for men to lie.
Yet now, I charge thee, quickly go again
As thou art lief and dear, and do the thing
I bad thee, watch, and lightly bring me word."

    Then went Sir Bedivere the second time
Across the ridge, and paced beside the mere,
Counting the dewy pebbles, fix'd in thought;
But when he saw the wonder of the hilt,
How curiously and strangely chased, he smote
His palms together, and he cried aloud,
    "And if indeed I cast the brand away,
Surely a precious thing, one worthy note,
Should thus be lost for ever from the earth,
Which might have pleased the eyes of many men.
What good should follow this, if this were done?
What harm, undone? deep harm to disobey,
Seeing obedience is the bond of rule.
Were it well to obey then, if a king demand
An act unprofitable, against himself?
The King is sick, and knows not what he does.
What record, or what relic of my lord
Should be to aftertime, but empty breath
And rumours of a doubt? but were this kept,
Stored in some treasure-house of mighty kings.
Some one might show it at a joust of arms,
Saying, 'King Arthur's sword, Excalibur,
Wrought by the lonely maiden of the Lake.
Nine years she wrought it, sitting in the deeps
Upon the hidden bases of the hills.'
So might some old man speak in the aftertime
To all the people, winning reverence.
But now much honour and much fame were lost."
    So spake he, clouded with his own conceit,
And hid Excalibur the second time,
And so strode back slow to the wounded King.
    Then spoke King Arthur, breathing heavily:
"What is it thou hast seen? or what hast heard?"
    And answer made the bold Sir Bedivere:
"I heard the water lapping on the crag,
And the long ripple washing in the reeds."
    To whom replied King Arthur, much in wrath:
"Ah, miserable and unkind, untrue,
Unknightly, traitor-hearted! Woe is me!
Authority forgets a dying king,
Laid widow'd of the power in his eye
That bow'd the will. I see thee what thou art,
For thou, the latest-left of all my knights,
In whom should meet the offices of all,
Thou wouldst betray me for the precious hilt;

Either from lust of gold, or like a girl
Valuing the giddy pleasure of the eyes.
Yet, for a man may fail in duty twice,
And the third time may prosper, get thee hence:
But, if thou spare to fling Excalibur,
I will arise and slay thee with my hands."
    Then quickly rose Sir Bedivere, and ran,
And, leaping down the ridges lightly, plunged
Among the bulrush-beds, and clutch'd the sword,
And strongly wheel'd and threw it. The great brand
Made lightnings in the splendour of the moon,
And flashing round and round, and whirl'd in an arch,
Shot like a streamer of the northern morn,
Seen where the moving isles of winter shock
By night, with noises of the northern sea.
So flash'd and fell the brand Excalibur:
But ere he dipt the surface, rose an arm
Clothed in white samite, mystic, wonderful,
And caught him by the hilt, and brandish'd him
Three times, and drew him under in the mere.
And lightly went the other to the King.

    Then spoke King Arthur, drawing thicker breath:
"Now see I by thine eyes that this is done.
Speak out: what is it thou hast heard, or seen?"
    And answer made the bold Sir Bedivere:
"Sir King, I closed mine eyelids, lest the gems
Should blind my purpose, for I never saw,
Nor shall see, here or elsewhere, till I die,
Not tho' I live three lives of mortal men,
So great a miracle as yonder hilt.
Then with both hands I flung him, wheeling him;
But when I look'd again, behold an arm,
Clothed in white samite, mystic, wonderful,
That caught him by the hilt, and brandish'd him
Three times, and drew him under in the mere."
    And answer made King Arthur, breathing hard:
"My end draws nigh; 'tis time that I were gone.
Make broad thy shoulders to receive my weight,
And bear me to the margin; yet I fear
My wound hath taken cold, and I shall die."
    So saying, from the pavement he half rose,
Slowly, with pain, reclining on his arm,
And looking wistfully with wide blue eyes
As in a picture. Him Sir Bedivere
Remorsefully regarded thro' his tears,
And would have spoken, but he found not words,

Then took with care, and kneeling on one knee,
O'er both his shoulders drew the languid hands,
And rising bore him thro' the place of tombs.

But, as he walk'd, King Arthur panted hard,
Like one that feels a nightmare on his bed
When all the house is mute. So sigh'd the King,
Muttering and murmuring at his ear, "Quick, quick!
I fear it is too late, and I shall die."
But the other swiftly strode from ridge to ridge,
Clothed with his breath, and looking, as he walk'd,
Larger than human on the frozen hills.
He heard the deep behind him, and a cry
Before. His own thought drove him, like a goad.
Dry clash'd his harness in the icy caves
And barren chasms, and all to left and right
The bare black cliff clang'd round him, as he based
His feet on juts of slippery crag that rang
Sharp-smitten with the dint of armed heels—
And on a sudden, lo! the level lake,
And the long glories of the winter moon.

Then saw they how there hove a dusky barge,
Dark as a funeral scarf from stem to stern,
Beneath them; and descending they were ware
That all the decks were dense with stately forms

Black-stoled, black-hooded, like a dream – by these
Three Queens with crowns of gold – and from them rose
A cry that shiver'd to the tingling stars,
And, as it were one voice an agony
Of lamentation, like a wind, that shrills
All night in a waste land, where no one comes,
Or hath come, since the making of the world.

Then murmur'd Arthur, "Place me in the barge,"
And to the barge they came. There those three Queens
Put forth their hands, and took the King, and wept.
But she, that rose the tallest of them all
And fairest, laid his head upon her lap,
And loosed the shatter'd casque, and chafed his hands,
And call'd him by his name, complaining loud,
And dropping bitter tears against his brow
Striped with dark blood: for all his face was white
And colourless, and like the wither'd moon
Smote by the fresh beam of the springing east;

And all his greaves and cuisses dash'd with drops
Of onset; and the light and lustrous curls–
That made his forehead like a rising sun
High from the dias-throne – were parch'd with dust;
Or, clotted into points and hanging loose,
Mix'd with the knightly growth that fringed his lips.
So like a shatter'd column lay the King;
Not like that Arthur who, with lance in rest,
From spur to plume a star of tournament,
Shot thro' the lists at Camelot, and charged
Before the eyes of ladies and of kings.
   Then loudly cried the bold Sir Bedivere,
"Ah! my Lord Arthur, whither shall I go?
Where shall I hide my forehead and my eyes?
For now I see the true old times are dead,
When every morning brought a noble chance,
And every chance brought out a noble knight.
Such times have been not since the light that led
The holy Elders with the gift of myrrh.
But now the whole ROUND TABLE is dissolved
Which was an image of the mighty world;
And I, the last, go forth companionless,
And the days darken round me, and the years,
Among new men, strange faces, other minds."

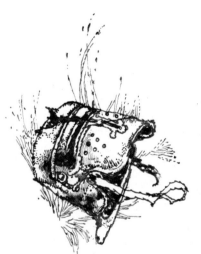

   And slowly answered Arthur from the barge:
"The old order changeth, yielding place to new,
And God fulfils Himself in many ways,
Lest one good custom should corrupt the world.
Comfort thyself: what comfort is in me?
I have lived my life, and that which I have done
May He within Himself make pure! but thou,
If thou shouldst never see my face again,
Pray for my soul. More things are wrought by prayer
Than this world dreams of. Wherefore, let thy voice
Rise like a fountain for me night and day.
For what are men better than sheep or goats
That nourish a blind life within the brain,
If, knowing God, they lift not hands of prayer
Both for themselves and those who call them friend?
For so the whole round earth is every way
Bound by gold chains about the feet of God.
But now farewell. I am going a long way
With these thou seëst – if indeed I go–
(For all my mind is clouded with a doubt)
To the island-valley of Avilion;
Where falls not hail, or rain, or any snow,
Nor ever wind blows loudly; but it lies
Deep-meadow'd, happy, fair with orchard-lawns
And bowery hollows crown'd with summer sea,
Where I will heal me of my grievous wound."
   So said he, and the barge with oar and sail
Moved from the brink, like some fullbreasted swan
That, fluting a wild carol ere her death,
Ruffles her pure cold plume, and takes the flood
With swarthy webs. Long stood Sir Bedivere
Revolving many memories, till the hull
Look'd one black dot against the verge of dawn,
And on the mere the wailing died away.
King Arthur, like a modern gentleman
Of stateliest port; and all the people cried,
"Arthur is come again: he cannot die."
Then those that stood upon the hills behind
Repeated – "Come again, and thrice as fair;"
And, further inland, voices echo'd – "Come
With all good things, and war shall be no more."
At this a hundred bells began to peal,
That with the sound I woke, and heard indeed
The clear church-bells ring in the Christmas morn.

ALFRED, LORD TENNYSON

Anthem for Doomed Youth

What passing-bells for these who die as cattle?
    Only the monstrous anger of the guns.
Only the stuttering rifles' rapid rattle
    Can patter out their hasty orisons.
No mockeries now for them; no prayers nor bells,
    Nor any voice of mourning save the choirs,–
The shrill, demented choirs of wailing shells;
    And bugles calling for them from sad shires.

What candles may be held to speed them all?
    Not in the hands of boys, but in their eyes
    Shall shine the holy glimmers of good-byes.
The pallor of girls' brows shall be their pall;
    Their flowers the tenderness of patient minds,
    And each slow dusk a drawing-down of blinds.

WILFRED OWEN

ALL THINGS BRIGHT AND BEAUTIFUL...

in between these sheets are pressed
not only flowers
but all the rest of nature
nearly

Birches

When I see birches bend to left and right
Across the lines of straighter darker trees,
I like to think some boy's been swinging them.
But swinging doesn't bend them down to stay
As ice-storms do. Often you must have seen them
Loaded with ice a sunny winter morning
After a rain. They click upon themselves
As the breeze rises, and turn many-coloured
As the stir cracks and crazes their enamel.
Soon the sun's warmth makes them shed crystal shell
Shattering and avalanching on the snow-crust —
Such heaps of broken glass to sweep away
You'd think the inner dome of heaven had fallen.
They are dragged to the withered bracken by the load,
And they seem not to break; though once they are bowed
So low for long, they never right themselves:
You may see their trunks arching in the woods
Years afterwards, trailing their leaves on the ground
Like girls on hands and knees that throw their hair
Before them over their heads to dry in the sun.
But I was going to say when Truth broke in
With all her matter-of-fact about the ice-storm
I should prefer to have some boy bend them
As he went out and in to fetch the cows—
Some boy too far from town to learn baseball,
Whose only play was what he found himself,
Summer or winter, and could play alone.
One by one he subdued his father's trees
By riding them down over and over again
Until he took the stiffness out of them,

And not one but hung limp, not one was left
For him to conquer. He learned all there was
To learn about not launching out too soon
And so not carrying the tree away
Clear to the ground. He always kept his poise
To the top branches, climbing carefully
With the same pains you use to fill a cup
Up to the brim, and even above the brim.
Then he flung outward, feet first, with a swish,
Kicking his way down through the air to the ground.
So was I once myself a swinger of birches.
And so I dream of going back to be.
It's when I'm weary of considerations,
And life is too much like a pathless wood
Where your face burns and tickles with the cobwebs
Broken across it, and one eye is weeping
From a twig's having lashed across it open.
I'd like to get away from earth awhile
And then come back to it and begin over.
May no fate wilfully misunderstand me
And half grant what I wish and snatch me away
Not to return. Earth's the right place for love:
I don't know where it's likely to go better.
I'd like to go by climbing a birch tree
And climb black branches up a snow-white trunk
Toward heaven, till the tree could bear no more,
But dipped its top and set me down again.
That would be good both going and coming back.
One could do worse than be a swinger of birches.

ROBERT FROST

Daffodils

I wandered lonely as a cloud
    That floats on high o'er vales and hills,
When all at once I saw a crowd,
    A host, of golden daffodils;
Beside the lake, beneath the trees,
Fluttering and dancing in the breeze.

Continuous as the stars that shine
    And twinkle on the Milky Way,
They stretched in never-ending line
    Along the margin of a bay:
Ten thousand saw I at a glance,
Tossing their heads in sprightly dance.

The waves beside them danced, but they
    Out-did the sparkling waves in glee:
A poet could not but be gay,
    In such a jocund company:
I gazed – and gazed – but little thought
What wealth the show to me had brought:

For oft, when on my couch I lie
    In vacant or in pensive mood,
They flash upon that inward eye
    Which is the bliss of solitude;
And then my heart with pleasure fills,
And dances with the daffodils.

WILLIAM WORDSWORTH

Binsey Poplars

My aspens dear, whose airy cages quelled,
Quelled or quenched in leaves the leaping sun,
All felled, felled, are all felled;
    Of a fresh and following folded rank
          Not spared, not one
          That dandled a sandalled
    Shadow that swam or sank
On meadow and river and wind-wandering
weed-winding bank.

O if we but knew what we do
         When we delve or hew—
    Hack and rack the growing green!
         Since country is so tender
To touch, her being so slender,
That, like this sleek and seeing ball
But a prick will make no eye at all,
Where we, even where we mean
         To mend her we end her,
        When we hew or delve:
After-comers cannot guess the beauty been.
Ten or twelve, only ten or twelve
    Strokes of havoc unselve
        The sweet especial scene,
    Rural scene, a rural scene,
    Sweet especial rural scene.

GERARD MANLEY HOPKINS

A Red, Red Rose

My love is like a red, red rose
 That's newly sprung in June:
My love is like the melody
 That's sweetly played in tune.

As fair art thou, my bonnie lass,
 So deep in love am I:
And I will love thee still, my dear,
 Till a' the seas gang dry.

Till a' the seas gang dry, my dear,
 And the rocks melt wi' the sun:
And I will love thee still, my dear,
 While the sands o' life shall run.

And fare thee weel, my only love,
 And fare thee weel a while!
And I will come again, my love,
 Thou' it were ten thousand mile.

ROBERT BURNS

The Darkening Garden

Where have all the colours gone?

Red of roses, green of grass,
Brown of tree-trunk, gold of cowslip,
Pink of poppy, blue of cornflower,
Who among you saw them pass?

They have gone to make the sunset:

Broidered on the western sky,
All the colours of our garden,
Woven into a lovely curtain,
Over the bed where Day doth die.

UNKNOWN

Flint

An emerald is as green as grass,
    A ruby red as blood;
A sapphire shines as blue as heaven;
    A flint lies in the mud.

A diamond is a brilliant stone,
    To catch the world's desire;
An opal holds a fiery spark;
    But a flint holds fire.

CHRISTINA ROSSETTI

Cargoes

Quinquireme of Nineveh from distant Ophir
Rowing home to haven in sunny Palestine,
With a cargo of ivory,
And apes and peacocks,
Sandalwood, cedarwood, and sweet white wine.

Stately Spanish galleon coming from the Isthmus,
Dipping through the Tropics by the palm-green shores,
With a cargo of diamonds,
Emeralds, amethysts,
Topazes, and cinnamon, and gold moidores.

Dirty British coaster with a salt-caked smoke stack
Butting through the Channel in the mad March days,
With a cargo of Tyne coal,
Road-rail, pig-lead,
Firewood, iron-ware, and cheap tin trays.

JOHN MASEFIELD

103

Sea-Fever

I must down to the seas again, to the lonely sea and the sky,
And all I ask is a tall ship and a star to steer her by,
And the wheel's kick and the wind's song and the white sail's shaking,
And a grey mist on the sea's face and a grey dawn breaking.

I must down to the seas again, for the call of the running tide
Is a wild call and a clear call that may not be denied;
And all I ask is a windy day with the white clouds flying,
And the flung spray and the blown spume, and the seagulls crying.

I must down to the seas again to the vagrant gypsy life.
To the gull's way and the whale's way where the wind's like a whetted knife;
And all I ask is a merry yarn from a laughing fellow-rover,
And quiet sleep and a sweet dream when the long trick's over.

JOHN MASEFIELD

Morning after a Storm

There was a roaring in the wind all night;
The rain came heavily and fell in floods;
But now the sun is rising calm and bright;
The birds are singing in the distant woods;
Over his own sweet voice the stock-dove broods;
The Jay makes answer as the Magpie chatters;
And all the air is filled with pleasant noise of waters.

All things that love the sun are out of doors;
The sky rejoices in the morning's birth;
The grass is bright with rain-drops – on the moors
The hare is running races in her mirth;
And with her feet she from the plashy earth
Raises a mist, that, glittering in the sun,
Runs with her all the way, wherever she doth run.

WILLIAM WORDSWORTH

The Lake Isle of Innisfree

I will arise and go now, and go to Innisfree,
And a small cabin build there, of clay and wattles made:
Nine bean-rows will I have there, a hive for the honey-bee,
And live alone in the bee-loud glade.

And I shall have some peace there, for peace comes dropping slow,
Dropping from the veils of the morning to where the cricket sings;
There midnight's all a glimmer, and noon a purple glow,
And evening full of the linnet's wings.

I will arise and go now, for always night and day
I hear lake water lapping with low sounds by the shore;
While I stand on the roadway, or on the pavements grey,
I hear it in the deep heart's core.

W. B. YEATS

Leisure

What is this life if, full of care,
We have no time to stand and stare.

No time to stand beneath the boughs
And stare as long as sheep or cows.

No time to see, when woods we pass,
Where squirrels hide their nuts in grass.

No time to see, in broad daylight,
Streams full of stars like skies at night.

No time to turn at Beauty's glance,
And watch her feet, how they can dance.

No time to wait till her mouth can
Enrich that smile her eyes began.

A poor life this if, full of care,
We have no time to stand and stare.

W. H. DAVIES

...ALL CREATURES GREAT AND SMALL

nature nature
we don't hature
and none of the animals are in cages
they're all in the following pages

The Tyger

Tyger! Tyger! burning bright
In the forests of the night,
What immortal hand or eye
Could frame thy fearful symmetry?

In what distant deeps or skies
Burnt the fire of thine eyes?
On what wings dare he aspire?
What the hand dare seize the fire?

And what shoulder, & what art,
Could twist the sinews of thy heart?
And when thy heart began to beat,
What dread hand? & what dread feet?

What the hammer? what the chain?
In what furnace was thy brain?
What the anvil? what dread grasp
Dare its deadly terrors clasp?

When the stars threw down their spears,
And water'd heaven with their tears,
Did he smile his work to see?
Did he who made the Lamb make thee?

Tyger! Tyger! burning bright
In the forests of the night,
What immortal hand or eye,
Dare frame thy fearful symmetry?

WILLIAM BLAKE

The Rum Tum Tugger

The Rum Tum Tugger is a Curious Cat:
If you offer him pheasant he would rather have grouse.
If you put him in a house he would much prefer a flat,
If you put him in a flat then he'd rather have a house.
If you set him on a mouse then he only wants a rat,
If you set him on a rat then he'd rather chase a mouse.
Yes the Rum Tum Tugger is a Curious Cat—
　　And there isn't any call for me to shout it:
　　　　For he will do
　　　　As he do do
　　　　　　And there's no doing anything about it!

The Rum Tum Tugger is a terrible bore:
When you let him in, then he wants to be out;
He's always on the wrong side of every door,
And as soon as he's at home, then he'd like to get about.
He likes to lie in the bureau drawer,
But he makes such a fuss if he can't get out.
Yes the Rum Tum Tugger is a Curious Cat—
    And it isn't any use for you to doubt it:
        For he will do
        As he do do
            And there's no doing anything about it!

The Rum Tum Tugger is a curious beast:
His disobliging ways are a matter of habit.
If you offer him fish then he always wants a feast;
When there isn't any fish then he won't eat rabbit.
If you offer him cream then he sniffs and sneers,
For he only likes what he finds for himself;
So you'll catch him in it right up to the ears,
If you put it away on the larder shelf.
The Rum Tum Tugger is artful and knowing,
The Rum Tum Tugger doesn't care for a cuddle;
But he'll leap on your lap in the middle of your sewing,
For there's nothing he enjoys like a horrible muddle.
Yes the Rum Tum Tugger is a Curious Cat—
    And there isn't any need for me to spout it.
        For he will do
        As he do do
            And there's no doing anything about it!

T. S. ELIOT

Roger the Dog

Asleep he wheezes at his ease.
He only wakes to scratch his fleas.

He hogs the fire, he bakes his head
As if it were a loaf of bread.

He's just a sack of snoring dog.
You can lug him like a log.

You can roll him with your foot,
He'll stay snoring where he's put.

I take him out for exercise,
He rolls in cowclap up to his eyes.

He will not race, he will not romp,
He saves his strength for gobble and chomp.

He'll work as hard as you could wish
Emptying his dinner dish,

Then flops flat, and digs down deep,
Like a miner, into sleep.

TED HUGHES

114

Cats

Cats sleep
Anywhere,
Any table,
Any chair,
Top of piano,
Window-ledge,
In the middle,
On the edge,
Open drawer,
Empty shoe,
Anybody's
Lap will do,
Fitted in a
Cardboard box,
In the cupboard
With your frocks
Anywhere!
They don't care!
Cats sleep
Anywhere.

ELEANOR FARJEON

The Terns

Said the mother Tern
    to her baby Tern
Would you like a brother?
Said baby Tern
    to mother Tern
Yes
One good Tern deserves another.

SPIKE MILLIGAN

The Cow

The cow is of the bovine ilk;
One end is moo, the other, milk.

OGDEN NASH

Our Doggy

First he sat, and then he lay,
And then he said: I've come to stay.
And that is how we acquired our doggy Pontz.
He is all right as dogs go, but not quite what one wants.
Because he talks. He talks like you and me.
And he is not you and me, he is made differently.
You think it is nice to have a talking animal?
It is not nice. It is unnatural.

STEVIE SMITH

The Shark

A treacherous monster is the Shark,
He never makes the least remark.

And when he sees you on the sand,
He doesn't seem to want to land.

He watches you take off your clothes,
And not the least excitement shows.

His eyes do not grow bright or roll,
He has astounding self-control.

He waits till you are quite undressed,
And seems to take no interest.

And when towards the sea you leap,
He looks as if he were asleep.

But when you once get in his range,
His whole demeanor seems to change.

He throws his body right about,
And his true character comes out.

It's no use crying or appealing,
He seems to lose all decent feeling.

After this warning you will wish
To keep clear of this treacherous fish.

His back is black, his stomach white,
He has a very dangerous bite.

LORD ALFRED DOUGLAS

A Considerable Speck

(MICROSCOPIC)

A speck that would have been beneath my sight
On any but a paper sheet so white
Set off across what I had written there.
And I had idly poised my pen in air
To stop it with a period of ink
When something strange about it made me think.
This was no dust speck by my breathing blown,
But unmistakably a living mite
With inclinations it could call its own.
It paused as with suspicion of my pen,
And then came racing wildly on again
To where my manuscript was not yet dry;
Then paused again and either drank or smelt-
With loathing, for again it turned to fly.
Plainly with an intelligence I dealt.
It seemed too tiny to have room for feet,
Yet must have had a set of them complete
To express how much it didn't want to die
It ran with terror and with cunning crept.
It faltered: I could see it hesitate;
Then in the middle of the open sheet
Cower down in desperation to accept
Whatever I accorded it of fate.
I have none of the tenderer-than-thou
Collectivistic regimenting love
With which the modern world is being swept.
But this poor microscopic item now
Since it was nothing I knew evil of
I let it lie there till I hope it slept.

I have a mind myself and recognize
Mind when I meet with it in any guise.
No one can know how glad I am to find
On any sheet the least display of mind.

ROBERT FROST

Downside-up

A vampire bat,
Of great renown,
Was known the world over,
To hang up and not down.

At blood-drinking orgies,
Where bats came to sup,
They marvelled at him who,
Hung not down but up.

In every church belfry,
In village and town,
Bats feted their fellow,
Who hung up and not down.

Crying "Raise high your glasses,
And drain every cup,
Here's health to the bat,
That hangs not down but up!"

WILLIS HALL

Snake

A snake came to my water-trough
On a hot, hot day, and I in pyjamas for the heat,
To drink there.

In the deep, strange-scented shade of the great dark carob-tree
I came down the steps with my pitcher
And must wait, must stand and wait, for there he was at the trough before me.

He reached down from a fissure in the earth-wall in the gloom
And trailed his yellow-brown slackness soft-bellied down, over the edge of the stone trough
And rested his throat upon the stone bottom,
And where the water had dripped from the tap, in a small clearness,
He sipped with his straight mouth,
Softly drank through his straight gums, into his slack long body,
Silently.

Someone was before me at my water-trough,
And I, like a second comer, waiting.

He lifted his head from his drinking, as cattle do,
And looked at me vaguely, as drinking cattle do,
And flickered his two-forked tongue from his lips, and mused a moment,
And stooped and drank a little more,
Being earth-brown, earth-golden from the burning bowels of the earth
On the day of Sicilian July, with Etna smoking.

The voice of my education said to me
He must be killed,
For in Sicily the black, black snakes are innocent, the gold are venomous.

And voices in me said, If you were a man
You would take a stick and break him now, and finish him off.

But must I confess how I liked him,
How glad I was he had come like a guest in quiet, to drink at my water-trough
And depart peaceful, pacified, and thankless,
Into the burning bowels of this earth?

Was it cowardice, that I dared not kill him?
Was it perversity, that I longed to talk to him?
Was it humility, to feel so honoured?
I felt so honoured.

And yet those voices:
If you were not afraid, you would kill him!

And truly I was afraid, I was most afraid,
But even so, honoured still more
That he should seek my hospitality
From out the dark door of the secret earth.

He drank enough
And lifted his head, dreamily, as one who has drunken,
And flickered his tongue like a forked night on the air, so black;
Seeming to lick his lips,
And looked around like a god, unseeing into the air,
And slowly turned his head,
And slowly, very slowly, as if thrice adream,
Proceeded to draw his slow length curving round
And climb again the broken bank of my wall-face.

And as he put his head into that dreadful hole,
And as he slowly drew up, snake-easing his shoulders, and entered farther,
A sort of horror, a sort of protest against his withdrawing into that horrid black hole,
Deliberately going into the blackness, and slowly drawing himself after,
Overcame me now his back was turned.

I looked round, I put down my pitcher,
I picked up a clumsy log
And threw it at the water-trough with a clatter.

I think it did not hit him,
But suddenly that part of him that was left behind convulsed in undignified haste,
Writhed like lightning, and was gone
Into the black hole, the earth-lipped fissure in the wall front,
At which, in the intense still noon, I stared with fascination.

And immediately I regretted it.
I thought how paltry, how vulgar, what a mean act!
I despised myself and the voices of my accursed human education.

And I thought of the albatross,
And I wished he would come back, my snake.

For he seemed to me again like a king,
Like a king in exile, uncrowned in the underworld,
Now due to be crowned again.

And so, I missed my chance with one of the lords
Of life.
And I have something to expiate;
A pettiness.   D. H. LAWRENCE

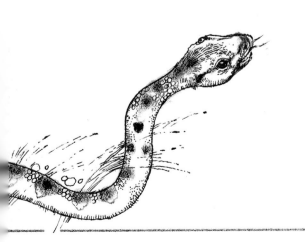
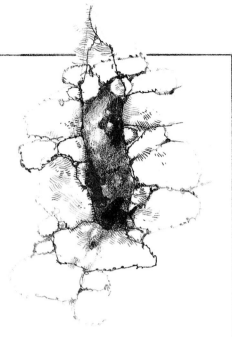

The Frog

Be kind and tender to the Frog,
   And do not call him names,
As "Slimy skin," or "Polly-wog,"
   Or likewise "Ugly James,"
Or "Gape-a-grin," or "Toad-gone-wrong,"
   Or "Billy Bandy-knees":
The Frog is justly sensitive
   To epithets like these.
No animal will more repay
   A treatment kind and fair;
At least so lonely people say
Who keep a frog (and, by the way,
   They are extremely rare).

HILAIRE BELLOC

Ducks' Ditty

All along the backwater,
Through the rushes tall,
Ducks are a-dabbling,
Up tails all!

Ducks' tails, drakes' tails,
Yellow feet a-quiver,
Yellow bills all out of sight
Busy in the river!

Slushy green undergrowth
Where the roach swim –
Here we keep our larder,
Cool and full and dim.

Everyone for what he likes!
We like to be
Heads down, tails up,
Dabbling free!

High in the blue above
Swifts whirl and call –
We are down a-dabbling,
Up tails all!

KENNETH GRAHAME

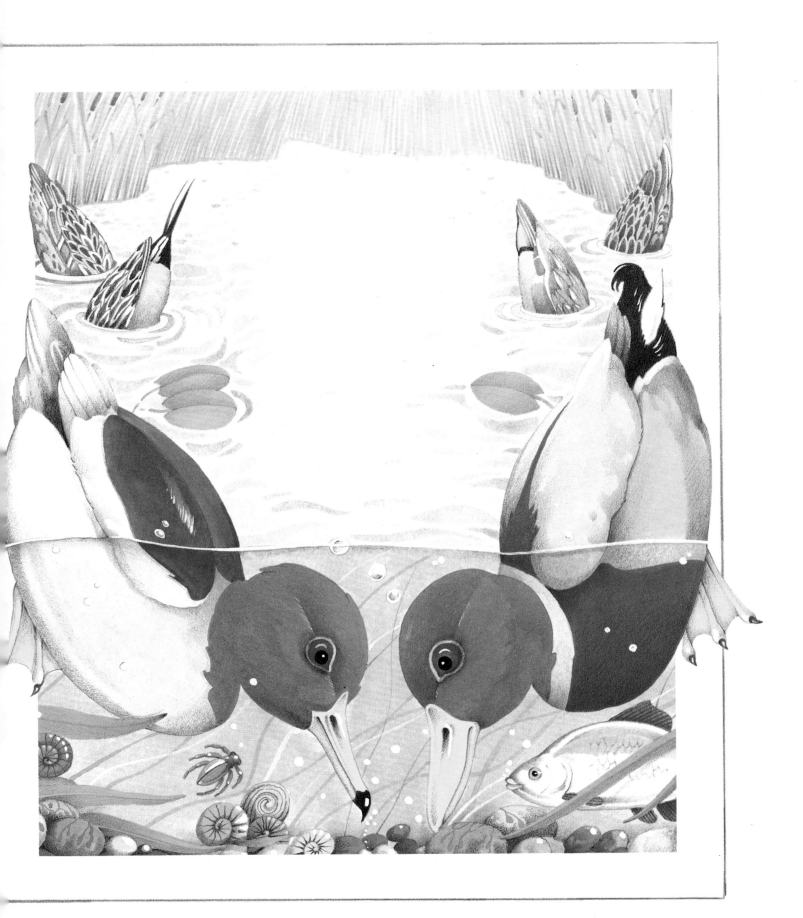

The Donkey

When fishes flew and forests walked
   And figs grew upon thorn,
Some moment when the moon was blood
   Then surely I was born;

With monstrous head and sickening cry
   And ears like errant wings,
The devil's walking parody
   On all four-footed things.

The tattered outlaw of the earth,
   Of ancient crooked will;
Starve, scourge, deride me: I am dumb,
   I keep my secret still.

Fools! For I also had my hour;
   One far fierce hour and sweet:
There was a shout about my ears,
   And palms before my feet.

G. K. CHESTERTON

The Fieldmouse

Where the acorn tumbles down,
  Where the ash tree sheds its berry,
With your fur so soft and brown,
  With your eye so round and merry,
Scarcely moving the long grass,
Fieldmouse, I can see you pass.

Little thing, in what dark den,
  Lie you all the winter sleeping?
Till warm weather comes again,
  Then once more I see you peeping
Round about the tall tree roots,
Nibbling at their fallen fruits.

Fieldmouse, fieldmouse, do not go,
  Where the farmer stacks his treasure,
Find the nut that falls below,
  Eat the acorn at your pleasure,
But you must not steal the grain
He has stacked with so much pain.

Make your hole where mosses spring,
  Underneath the tall oak's shadow,
Pretty, quiet, harmless thing,
  Play about the sunny meadow.
Keep away from corn and house,
None will harm you, little mouse.

CECIL FRANCES ALEXANDER

The Cow

The friendly cow, all red and white,
    I love with all my heart:
She gives me cream with all her might,
    To eat with apple-tart.

She wanders lowing here and there,
    And yet she cannot stray,
All in the pleasant open air
    The pleasant light of day,

And blown by all the winds that pass
    And wet with all the showers,
She walks among the meadow grass
    And eats the meadow flowers.

ROBERT LOUIS STEVENSON

The Owl and the Pussy-Cat

The Owl and the Pussy-cat went to sea
    In a beautiful pea-green boat,
They took some honey, and plenty of money,
    Wrapped up in a five-pound note.
The Owl looked up to the stars above,
    And sang to a small guitar,
"O lovely Pussy! O Pussy, my love,
        What a beautiful Pussy you are,
                You are,
                You are!
What a beautiful Pussy you are!"

Pussy said to the Owl, "You elegant fowl!
    How charmingly sweet you sing!
O let us be married! too long we have tarried:
    But what shall we do for a ring?"
They sailed away, for a year and a day,
    To the land where the Bong-tree grows
And there in a wood a Piggy-wig stood
    With a ring at the end of his nose,
        His nose,
        His nose,
    With a ring at the end of his nose.

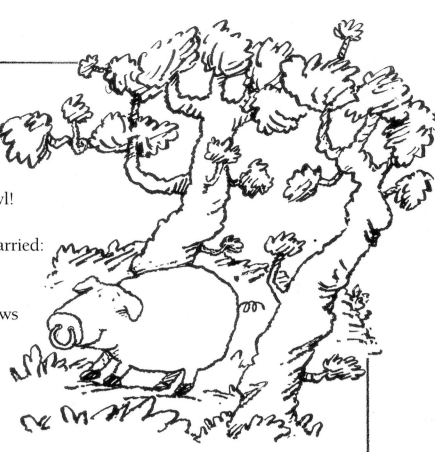

"Dear Pig, are you willing to sell for one shilling
    Your ring?" Said the Piggy, "I will."
So they took it away, and were married next day
    By the Turkey who lives on the hill.
They dined on mince, and slices of quince,
    Which they ate with a runcible spoon;
And hand in hand, on the edge of the sand,
    They danced by the light of the moon,
        The moon,
        The moon,
They danced by the light of the moon.

EDWARD LEAR

129

NEVER NEVER NONSENSE LAND

there was a young creature from space
who entered a three-legged race
he was not very fast
in fact he came last
because he was a bag of oven-ready chips

Father William

From "Alice's Adventures in Wonderland"

"You are old, Father William," the young man said,
    "And your hair has become very white;
And yet you incessantly stand on your head–
    Do you think, at your age, it is right?"

"In my youth," Father William replied to his son,
    "I feared it might injure the brain;
But now that I'm perfectly sure I have none,
    Why, I do it again and again."

"You are old," said the youth, "as I mentioned before,
    And have grown most uncommonly fat;
Yet you turned a back somersault in at the door–
    Pray, what is the reason of that?"

"In my youth," said the sage, as he shook his grey locks,
    "I kept all my limbs very supple.
By the use of this ointment – one shilling the box–
    Allow me to sell you a couple?"

"You are old," said the youth, "and your jaws are too weak
    For anything tougher than suet;
Yet you finished the goose, with the bones and the beak–
    Pray, how did you manage to do it?"

"In my youth," said his father, "I took to the law,
    And argued each case with my wife;
And the muscular strength which it gave to my jaw,
    Has lasted the rest of my life."

"You are old," said the youth, "one would hardly suppose
    That your eye was as steady as ever;
Yet you balanced an eel on the end of your nose–
    What made you so awfully clever?"

"I have answered three questions, and that is enough,"
    Said his father. "Don't give yourself airs!
Do you think I can listen all day to such stuff!
    Be off, or I'll kick you downstairs!"

LEWIS CARROLL

133

Alas, Poor Fred

Uncle Freddie bought a fly-trap,
Took it home and watered it,
Fed it flies and fertiliser,
Watched it growing bit by bit.
Until one day the fly-trap,
Took a shine to Uncle Fred,
Then BITE, MUNCH, CRUNCH,
GULP, SLURP and SWALLOW!
And poor old Uncle Fred was dead.

WILLIS HALL

134

The Revolt of the Lamp Posts

Last night I saw the lamp posts
That light up our back street
Wiggle, and then wriggle
And then, suddenly, they'd feet.

Then they all cleared off and left us,
The whole street in the dark,
So I left the house and followed,
There were millions in the park.

All the lamps from miles around
Had run away tonight,
They were dancing, they were singing,
And they held each other tight.

The king, a big green lamp post
Said "No more workin' brothers!
We'll leave them humings in the dark
And they'll bump into each other.

Just think about them walkin' round
With black eyes and broke noses
No more dogs to wet your feet
No more rusty toeses!

See, I've been a lamp post all me life, but
Now me mantles growin' dim,
They'll chuck me on the scrap heap
It's a shame! a crime! a sin!…"

The other lamp posts muttered
And began to hiss and boo,
"Let's march upon the Town Hall
That's what we ought to do!"

The Lord Mayor he was woken
By a terribobble sight,
When he opened up his window
Didn't he get a fright!

There were twenty million lamp posts
And the light as bright as day
And the young lamp posts were shoutin' out
"Free Speech and Equal Pay!–

New Mantles Every Quarter!"
"I agree" the Lord Mayor cried
"To everything you ask for!"
Then he quickly ran inside.

So I watched the lamp posts go back home,
As quickly as they came
And with the first light of the day,
They were in their holes again.

Now there's an old age home for lamp posts
And an old age pension scheme
And every month they're painted
With a coat of glossy green,

New mantles every couple of months,
And they stand up straighter too,
And only the Lord Mayor knows why,
Him, and me, and twenty million lamp posts,

And a couple hundred dogs – and you.

MIKE HARDING

From

The Bed Book

Beds come in all sizes –
Single or double,
Cot-size or cradle,
King-size or trundle.

Most Beds are Beds
For sleeping or resting,
But the *best* Beds are much
More interesting!

Not just a white little
Tucked-in-tight little
Nighty-night little
Turn-out-the-light little
Bed –

Instead
A Bed for Fishing,
A Bed for Cats,
A Bed for a Troupe of
Acrobats.

The *right* sort of Bed
(If you see what I mean)
Is a Bed that might
Be a Submarine

Nosing through water
Clear and green,
Silver and glittery
As a sardine

Or a Jet-Propelled Bed
For visiting Mars
With mosquito nets
For the shooting stars...

SYLVIA PLATH

The Jumblies

They went to sea in a Sieve, they did,
 In a Sieve they went to sea:
In spite of all their friends could say,
On a winter's morn, on a stormy day,
 In a Sieve they went to sea!
And when the Sieve turned round and round,
And everyone cried, "You'll all be drowned!"
They called aloud, "Our Sieve ain't big,
But we don't care a button! we don't care a fig!
 In a Sieve we'll go to sea!"
 Far and few, far and few,
 Are the lands where the Jumblies live;
Their heads are green, and their hands are blue,
 And they went to sea in a Sieve.

They sailed away in a Sieve, they did,
 In a Sieve they sailed so fast,
With only a beautiful pea-green veil
Tied with a riband by way of a sail,
 To a small tobacco-pipe mast;
And everyone said, who saw them go,
"O won't they be soon upset, you know!
For the sky is dark, and the voyage is long,
And happen what may, it's extremely wrong
 In a Sieve to sail so fast!"
 Far and few, far and few,
 Are the lands where the Jumblies live;
Their heads are green, and their hands are blue,
 And they went to sea in a Sieve.

The water it soon came in, it did,
   The water it soon came in;
So to keep them dry, they wrapped their feet
In a pinky paper all folded neat,
   And they fastened it down with a pin.
And they passed the night in a crockery-jar,
And each of them said, "How wise we are!
Though the sky be dark, and the voyage be long,
Yet we never can think we were rash or wrong,
   While round in our Sieve we spin!"
   Far and few, far and few,
   Are the lands where the Jumblies live;
Their heads are green, and their hands are blue,
   And they went to sea in a Sieve.

And all night long they sailed away;
   And when the sun went down,
They whistled and warbled a moony song
To the echoing sound of a coppery gong,
   In the shade of the mountains brown.
"O Timballo! How happy we are,
When we live in a Sieve and a crockery-jar,
And all night long in the moonlight pale,
We sail away with a pea-green sail,
   In the shade of the mountains brown!"
   Far and few, far and few,
   Are the lands where the Jumblies live;
Their heads are green, and their hands are blue,
   And they went to sea in a Sieve.

They sailed to the Western Sea, they did,
    To a land all covered with trees,
And they bought an Owl, and a useful Cart,
And a pound of Rice, and a Cranberry Tart,
    And a hive of silvery Bees.
And they bought a Pig, and some green Jack-daws,
And a lovely Monkey with lollipop paws,
And forty bottles of Ring-Bo-Ree,
    And no end of Stilton Cheese.
    Far and few, far and few,
    Are the lands where the Jumblies live;
Their heads are green, and their hands are blue,
    And they went to sea in a Sieve.

And in twenty years they all came back,
    In twenty years or more,
And everyone said, "How tall they've grown!
For they've been to the Lakes, and the Torrible Zone,
    And the hills of the Chankly Bore!"
And they drank their health and gave them a feast
Of dumplings made of beautiful yeast;
And everyone said, "If we only live,
We too will go to sea in a Sieve, –

To the hills of the Chankly Bore!"
    Far and few, far and few,
    Are the lands where the Jumblies live;
Their heads are green, and their hands are blue,
    And they went to sea in a Sieve.

EDWARD LEAR

142

The Tree Hippopotamus

What do I know
    of the tree hippopotamus?
Well, I know a bit
    but not a whole lottamus.
I know that it sleeps
    in the Goolingey trees.
Where it hangs by its tail
    and it swings in the breeze.
And the Goolingey trees
    creak and strain from its weight,
And this is the reason
    they're never quite straight.
Which is why we should run when we
    see the great 'potamus
Lest he should wake up –
    and fall down ontopofus!

DOM MANSELL

Song of the Witches

From "Macbeth"

Double, double toil and trouble;
Fire burn and caldron bubble.

Fillet of a fenny snake,
In the caldron boil and bake;
Eye of newt and toe of frog,
Wool of bat and tongue of dog,
Adder's fork and blind-worm's sting,
Lizard's leg and howlet's wing,
For a charm of powerful trouble,
Like a hell-broth boil and bubble.

Double, double toil and trouble;
Fire burn and caldron bubble.
Cool it with a baboon's blood,
Then the charm is firm and good.

WILLIAM SHAKESPEARE

144

Some One

Some one came knocking
   At my wee, small door;
Some one came knocking,
   I'm sure – sure – sure;
I listened, I opened,
   I looked to left and right,
But naught there was a-stirring
   In the still dark night;
Only the busy beetle
   Tap-tapping in the wall,
Only from the forest
   The screech-owl's call,
Only the cricket whistling
   While the dewdrops fall,
So I know not who came knocking,
   At all, at all, at all.

WALTER DE LA MARE

Good Morning, Mr Croco-doco-dile

Good morning, Mr Croco-doco-dile,
And how are you today?
I like to see you croco-smoco-smile
In your croco-woco-way.

From the tip of your beautiful croco-toco-tail
To your croco-hoco-head
You seem to me so croco-stoco-still
As if you're croco-doco-dead.

Perhaps if I touch your croco-cloco-claw
Or your croco-snoco-snout,
Or get up close to your croco-joco-jaw
I shall very soon find out.

But suddenly I croco-soco-see
In your croco-oco-eye
A curious kind of croco-gloco-gleam,
So I just don't think I'll try.

Forgive me, Mr Croco-doco-dile
But it's time I was away.
Let's talk a little croco-woco-while
Another croco-doco-day.

CHARLES CAUSLEY

Of Pygmies, Palms and Pirates

Of pygmies, palms and pirates,
Of islands and lagoons,
Of blood-bespotted frigates,
Of crags and octoroons,
Of whales and broken bottles,
Of quicksands cold and grey,
Of ullages and dottles,
I have no more to say.

Of barley, corn and furrows,
Of farms and turf that heaves
Above such ghostly burrows
As twitch on summer eves
Of fallow-land and pasture,
Of skies both pink and grey,
I made a statement last year
And have no more to say.

MERVYN PEAKE

INDEX
OF TITLES AND FIRST LINES

THE POETS

ALDIS, Dorothy (modern, British)
ALEXANDER, Cecil Frances (1818-95, British)

BELLOC, Hilaire (1870-1953, Anglo/French)
BLAKE, William (1757-1827, British)
BODECKER, N.M. (modern, American)
BROOKE, Rupert (1887-1915, British)
BROWNING, Robert (1812-89, British)
BURNS, Robert (1759-96, British)
BYRON, Lord George (1788-1824, British)

CARROLL, Lewis (1832-98, British)
CAUSLEY, Charles (b 1917, British)
CHESTERTON, Gilbert Keith (1874-1936, British)
CLARE, John (1793-1864, British)
COLERIDGE, Samuel Taylor (1722-1834, British)
CUMMINGS, Edward Estlin (1894-1962, American)

DAHL, Roald (b 1916, British)
DAVIES, William Henry (1871-1940, British)
DE LA MARE, Walter (1873-1956, British)
DOUGLAS, Lord Alfred (1870-1945, British)
DUGAN, Michael (b 1947, Australian)

ELIOT, Thomas Stearns (1888-1965, American)

FARJEON, Eleanor (1881-1965, British)
FIELD, Rachel (1894-1942, American)
FROST, Robert Lee (1874-1963, American)

GRAHAME, Kenneth (1859-1932, British)
GRAVES, Robert von Ranke (1895-1985, British)

HALL, Willis (b 1929, British)
HARDING, Mike (modern, British)
HARDY, Thomas (1840-1928, British)
HEANEY, Seamus (b 1939, Irish)
HEGLEY, John (b 1953, British)
HOGG, James (1770-1835, British)
HOPKINS, Gerard Manley (1844-89, British)
HUGHES, Ted (b 1930, British, Poet Laureate)

KEATS, John (1795-1821, British)
KINGSLEY, Charles (1819-75, British)
KIPLING, Rudyard (1865-1936, British)

LAWRENCE, David Herbert (1885-1930, British)
LEAR, Edward (1812-88, British)
LENSKI, Lois (1893-1974, American)

LONGFELLOW, Henry Wadsworth (1807-82, American)

MALORY, Sir Thomas (*d* 1471, British)
MANSELL, Dom (modern, British)
MASEFIELD, John Edward (1878-1967, British)
McGOUGH, Roger (*b* 1937, British)
MILLIGAN, Spike (*b* 1918, British)
MITCHELL, Adrian (*b* 1932, British)

NASH, Ogden (1902-71, American)

OWEN, Wilfred (1893-1918, British)

PATTEN, Brian (*b* 1946, British)
PEAKE, Mervyn (1911-68, British)
PLATH, Sylvia (1932-63, American)
POE, Edgar Allen (1809-49, American)

ROSSETTI, Christina Georgina (1830-94, British)

SHAKESPEARE, William (1564-1616, British)
SHELLEY, Percy Bysshe (1792-1822, British)
SMITH, Stevie (1902-71, British)
STEVENSON, Robert Louis (1850-94, British)

TENNYSON, Alfred Lord (1809-92, British)
TESSIMOND, A.S.J. (1902-62, British)
THOMAS, Edward (1878-1917, British)

WORDSWORTH, William (1770-1850, British)

YEATS, William Butler (1865-1939, Irish)
YEVTUSHENKO, Yevgeny (modern, Russian)

ACKNOWLEDGEMENTS

The publishers gratefully acknowledge permission to reproduce the following poems. The publishers have made every effort to trace copyright holders. If we have inadvertently omitted to acknowledge anyone, we should be most grateful if this could be brought to our attention for correction at the first opportunity.

DOROTHY ALDIS 'My Nose' reprinted by permission of G. P. Putnam's Sons from *All Together* by Dorothy Aldis, copyright 1925-1928, 1934, 1939, 1952 copyright renewed 1953-1956, 1962, 1967 by Dorothy Aldis.

HILAIRE BELLOC 'The Frog' from *The Bad Child's Book of Beasts* reprinted by permission of the publisher Gerald Duckworth & Co. Ltd.

N. BODECKER 'When All the World is Full of Snow' from *Hurry, Hurry Mary, Dear* reprinted by permission of N. Bodecker and the publisher J. M. Dent and Sons, Ltd.

CHARLES CAUSLEY 'Colonel Fazackerley' from *Figgie Hobbin* reprinted by permission of Charles Causley, the publisher Macmillan and David Higham Associates Ltd. 'Good Morning, Mr Croco-doco-dile' from *Early in the Morning* reprinted by permission of Charles Causley, the publisher Penguin Books Ltd and David Higham Associates Ltd.

E. E. CUMMINGS 'maggie and milly and mollie and may' reprinted by permission of Grafton Books, a division of William Collins and Sons.

ROALD DAHL 'Aunt Sponge and Aunt Spiker' from *James and the Giant Peach* by Roald Dahl, reprinted by permission of Unwin Hyman and Penguin Books Ltd.

W. H. DAVIES 'Leisure' from *The Collected Poems of W. H. Davies* reprinted by permission of The Executors of the W. H. Davies Estate and Jonathan Cape Ltd, publisher.

WALTER DE LA MARE 'Some One' reprinted by permission of The Literary Trustees of Walter de la Mare and The Society of Authors as their representative.

LORD ALFRED DOUGLAS 'The Shark' reprinted by permission of The Lord Alfred Douglas Literary Estate.

MICHAEL DUGAN 'Herbaceous Plodd' reprinted by permission of Michael Dugan and *Jump* magazine.

T. S. ELIOT 'The Rum Tum Tugger' reprinted by permission of Faber and Faber Ltd from *Old Possum's Book of Practical Cats* by T. S. Eliot.

ELEANOR FARJEON 'Apple Time' and 'Cats' reprinted by permission of the Oxford University Press from *The Children's Bells* by Eleanor Farjeon.

RACHEL FIELD 'Some People' reprinted with permission of Macmillan Publishing Company from *Poems* by Rachel Field (New York: Macmillan, 1957).

ROBERT FROST 'Stopping by Woods on a Snowy Evening', 'Birches' and 'A Considerable Speck' reprinted by permission of the Estate of Robert Frost and Jonathan Cape Ltd. from *The Poetry of Robert Frost* edited by Edward Connery Latham.

ROBERT GRAVES 'The Hero' reprinted by permission of A. P. Watt Limited on behalf of The Executors of the Estate of Robert Graves from *Collected Poems 1975* by Robert Graves.

WILLIS HALL 'Alas, Poor Fred', 'Believing', 'Celebration' and 'Downside Up' from *Spooky Rhymes* reprinted by permission of the author and The Hamlyn Publishing Group, a division of The Octopus Publishing Group Limited.

MIKE HARDING 'The Revolt of the Lamp Posts' reprinted by permission of Mike Harding and Moonraker Productions Ltd. from *Up the Boo Aye, Shooting Pookakies*.

SEAMUS HEANEY 'The Railway Children' reprinted by permission of Faber and Faber Ltd. from *Station Island* by Seamus Heaney.

JOHN HEGLEY 'Grandad's Glasses' and introductory poems reprinted by permission of the author.

TED HUGHES 'My Brother Bert' reprinted by permission of Faber and Faber Ltd. from *Meet My Folks* by Ted Hughes. 'Roger the Dog' reprinted by permission of Faber and Faber Ltd. from *What is the Truth?* by Ted Hughes.

LOIS LENSKI 'Sing a Song of People' from *The Life I Live* © 1965 The Lois Lenski Covey Foundation Inc.